atherine ♥ um .

xxxx

The Infamous
Bell Witch
of Tennessee

Charles Edwin Price

The Overmountain Press
JOHNSON CITY, TENNESSEE

ISBN 1-57072-008-8
Printed in the United States of America

1 2 3 4 5 6 7 8 9 0

For Melanie and Melissa
My two favorite people in the whole, wide world.
This one's for you!

Other books by Charles Edwin Price

Haints, Witches, and Boogers:
Tales from Upper East Tennessee

The Day They Hung The Elephant

Demon In The Woods:
Tall Tales and True from East Tennessee

The Mystery of Ghostly Vera
And Other Haunting Tales of Southwest Virginia

Haunted Jonesborough

I'd Rather Have A Talking Frog:
Tales From Johnson City

TABLE OF CONTENTS

INTRODUCTION

Come with me to meet "Kate," an unsavory creature from the other side of hell. Nearly two centuries ago she tortured a family unmercifully, finally killing its patriarch.

"Kate" is better known as the Bell Witch of Tennessee. As such, her name is forever linked with infamy. Even today, 177 years after she first appeared in Robertson County, Kate continues to hold some people in the town of Adams in a state of Draconian intimidation. Considering all the weird things that happen in and around Adams, there is strong reason to believe that Kate is still afoot in Robertson County, still tormenting the living.

Officially, the Bell Witch haunting is over. It ended about 1828 when Kate departed from the Bell family for the second time. Although she promised to return in 1935, 107 years later, she failed to show. At least none of the Bell descendants, much to their relief, reported seeing or hearing from her. Still, it's clear to some folks in Robertson County that the entire area continues to be bedeviled by something unexplainable.

The Bell Witch was the last thing the rabbit hunter and his friends thought of as they drove toward the Bell Witch Cave. On each side of the road lush, green fields spread out like a fluffy carpet under clear Tennessee skies. The fields looked so promising they seemed to have "rabbit" written all over them.

The hunter had driven only a short way when his car was suddenly lifted up and dumped onto its side. The stunned driver was sprawled against the side window, his surprised companions piled on top of him. After much scrambling and cursing, the hunters escaped the upended auto by wiggling through the passenger window.

Safely outside, they glanced around. There were no other vehicles on the road. Furthermore, nothing lying in the road could have thrown the car off balance enough to overturn the vehicle. Yet a heavy automobile doesn't take a notion to turn over by itself. Something *had* to be the cause. But what? To this day there is no logical explanation of what really happened.

Agnes Rippy, who works in the Robertson County Archives in Springfield, was born and raised in Robertson County. And like nearly everyone living there, she had heard Bell Witch stories all her life. In fact, this no-nonsense woman had heard *more than her share* and was getting sick and tired of the whole thing.

One day she went for a Sunday drive with her family. Her oldest son was driving the car, a practically new model. Since the road on which they were driving skirted Adams, the conversation naturally turned to the Bell Witch. Rippy decided she had heard enough witch talk.

"Everyone shut up!" she growled. "There's no such thing as the Bell Witch."

Instantly the car went dead and rolled to a stop.

Rippy's son got out and opened the hood. Nothing was wrong mechanically or electrically with the auto. It just wouldn't run.

And after that day *it never ran again.*

Rippy's son was forced to get another car.

He said to Rippy, "Mama, don't ever say there's no such thing as the Bell Witch again. Something happened to that car when you got to talking about it."

This book was written because of numerous requests from readers for me to tell the Bell Witch story. For a long time I thought the tale lay outside my territory. I was interested mainly in upper East Tennessee and Southwest Virginia ghost lore because, I felt, folklore collecting in those areas was sorely neglected.

I had heard about the Bell Witch when I was growing up near the tiny mill town of Ellicott City, Maryland. I had even read Charles Bailey Bell's apologetic family saga, *The Bell Witch: A Mysterious Spirit*, when I was in junior high school. But, at the time, I didn't consider the yarn anything more than a good ghost story.

Many outsiders who don't know a fig about Tennessee history do know a little something about three of its most famous squatters—David Crockett, Andrew Jackson, and the infamous Bell Witch. Even those native to the state who have spent their lives actively avoiding any contact with Tennessee history know about the witch. Few seem to tire of the story.

Readers picking up my earlier book *Haints, Witches, and Boogers: Tales from Upper East Tennessee* often ask if the Bell Witch story is included. I say no because *Haints* only contains ghost stories set in upper East Tennessee. But I began to hear so much about the Bell Witch that I had to find out more about her myself. (Throughout this book I often refer to the witch as a "her" because the spirit's gender is widely assumed to be female.)

Several books about the Bell Witch have already been written, scholarly papers solemnly composed, newspaper and magazine articles published, and films and TV shows produced. Legend and lore about the witch have been traded freely. But there was something missing in all this notoriety—something that piqued my interest beyond just recording another fascinating fragment of Tennessee folklore. The

Bell Witch was unlike any other supernatural creature I had ever written about—her influence more widespread, her legend more enduring. Furthermore, the spirit had actually killed a human being—poisoned him! And she is still supposed to be active.

Even though the Bell Witch has not been officially heard from since 1828—at least not that anyone knows of—her influence is still felt in Robertson County.

Charlie Willett, a prominent Springfield lawyer, was well liked in Robertson County. He was a direct descendant of the Bell family. Miss Cullen Gardner was a descendant of Joshua Gardner and worked at Randolph House.

Miss Gardner drove Mr. Willett to work every day, and each Christmas he bought her a new set of tires. They courted for years and were very much in love, but they believed that was as far as their romance could ever go.

All through the haunting, the Bell Witch had forbidden the marriage of their ancestors, Joshua Gardner and Betsy Bell. Betsy thought that ill would befall the couple if they ignored the witch, so she and Joshua went their separate ways.

Years later, it seems their descendants were also fearful of what the witch might do if the Bells and the Gardners were ever joined by marriage. Yolanda Reid, the Robertson County historian who knew both Gardner and Willett, said, "They courted up until the day he died—as old people. But they never married. They thought the witch's vindictiveness did not just apply to Betsy Bell or Joshua Gardner."

At this point the reader may think I mean to insinuate the people of Robertson County are backward or superstitious. *Nothing could be further from the truth. I want to make that quite clear at the very start.* But even the most stoic citizen cannot deny the odd things that happen almost daily in and around Adams. For example...

People snapping photographs around the Bell Witch Cave

are sometimes startled by what they find on their film after it has been developed. Shadows, splotches, shadowy figures, and even well-defined faces sometimes mysteriously appear.

Near the Bell Witch Cave parking lot is a large sinkhole, created when a portion of the Bell Witch Cave collapsed. Chris Kirby, one of the present owners of the cave, once photographed the sinkhole. On the finished color print appeared a wispy image that bore a startling resemblance to a devil-like face. The farther away the viewer stood from the picture, the more distinct the image became.

Is this the visage of the notorious Bell Witch?

This remarkable photo was taken of the sinkhole, just to the right of the Bell Witch Cave parking lot. The sinkhole was created when part of the Bell Witch Cave collapsed. When she took the photo, Chris Kirby said there was no mist in the sinkhole, but it showed up later when the film was processed. Some people who view the photo can discern a demonic face in the mist. Is this the face of the Bell Witch? (Photo courtesty of Walter and Chris Kirby)

Kirby has no explanation for why the image appeared on an otherwise routine photograph. She sent the print to a number of experts. They had no explanation either.

The skeptic would immediately declare that the photo was double exposed or caused by some defect in the camera or film. Fogging, which the picture immediately suggests, is common when using inexpensive cameras. But Kirby told me that similar images are regularly recorded on Polaroid film at the mouth of the Bell Witch Cave. It is virtually impossible to double expose a Polaroid snapshot.

Spirit photography is nothing new. In the latter part of the nineteenth century, so-called spirit photographs were popular. These photos were taken by mediums under normal conditions in studios. When the negative was processed, a second image would appear—that of a dead relative or close friend. The unexpected images were called "seconds."

Admittedly many spirit photographs were faked, products of skillful darkroom maneuvering. But there were also those not so easy to explain.

Traill Taylor was president of the Royal Photographic Society in England and a skeptic. At the height of the spirit photography craze, Taylor made it his business to take up spirit photography so that he could easily spot the fakes. He got a nasty surprise when his own photographs revealed unexplained images, in spite of his own best efforts to avoid them!

"The psychic figures behaved badly," he wrote in *Ghosts in Photographs*. "Some were in focus, others not so; some were lighted from the right, while the sitter was so from the left; some were comely, others not so; some monopolized the major portion of the plate, quite obliterating the material sitters; others were as if an atrociously badly vignetted portrait or one cut out of a photograph by a can opener, or equally badly clipped out or held up behind the sitter. But here is the point. Not one of these figures which came out so strongly in the negative was visible in any form or shape during the time of exposure in the camera."

For some reason, spiritual forces enjoy projecting themselves onto photographic film, to make their presence known to the living. The picture taken in the sinkhole by Chris Kirby, showing a mysterious image of an entity lurking there, may fall into this category.

Could it be the witch's way to announce to the world that she is, indeed, "alive" and well in Robertson County? It would be completely within her character to do just that!

Charles Edwin Price
Erwin, Tennessee
Winter 1994

Come, my heart, and let us try
   For a little season
Every burden to lay by.
   Come and let us reason.

What is this that casts you down?
   Who are those that grieve you?
Speak and let the worst be known.
   Speaking may relieve you.

Christ by faith I sometimes see,
   And He doth relieve me,
But my fears return again,
   These are they that grieve me.

Troubled like the restless sea,
   Feeble, faint and fearful,
Plagued with every sore disease,
   How can I be cheerful?

— A hymn sung by the Bell Witch of Tennessee
as quoted by Charles Bailey Bell

ACKNOWLEDGMENTS

I would like to express my appreciation to the following people. Without their help and encouragement, this book could not have been written.

First to Yolanda Reid, Robertson County historian, who spent time patiently explaining to me the ins and outs, whys and wherefores, of her county's history. Ms. Reid also volunteers her time in the Robertson County Archives, a wonderful repository of official court records reaching back to the beginning of Tennessee's statehood. The archive is a treasure trove for researchers.

To Mary Richards Sprouse, also an archive worker, who provided insights into the Bell Witch haunting and provided a number of wonderful stories from her own experience.

I would also like to thank Agnes Rippy of Springfield for her story about the witch and her son's automobile.

Nina Seeley provided valuable information on her brainchild, the "Bell Witch Opry."

To Chris Kirby, one of the owners of the Bell Witch Cave. Chris spent a couple of hours telling me about the strange things that have happened to her family and visitors, in and around the cave. She also lent valuable photographs to be reproduced in this book.

To the three dozen or so people who told me their own chilling experiences with the Bell Witch but asked that their names not be published, a heartfelt thanks. When telling personal "true" ghost stories, informants sometimes get a little publicity shy. Believe me, I totally understand where they're coming from.

To my editor at The Overmountain Press, Sherry Lewis, goes not only my thanks but my everlasting awe. So far she's wrestled through five of my books and, as far as I know, has not yet had to visit the funny farm for an extended stay.

And finally to the ever-patient Patty who, if she stays with me and puts up with my foolishness much longer, *will* end up on the funny farm.

To all these, and many more, thank you.

Charles Edwin Price

AUTHOR'S NOTE

Throughout this book I quote selections/dialogue liberally from two already published volumes: *The Bell Witch: A Mysterious Spirit* (1934) by Charles Bailey Bell and *The Bell Witch of Middle Tennessee* (1930) by Harriet Parks Miller. Since the authors of these books were supposedly assisted by Bell family members, I can only assume that the dialogue that they recorded is reasonably accurate. However, both books were written in Victorian-style prose. Some sentences seem to extend forever. Therefore, I have taken the liberty of repunctuating some of the original writing and substituting shorter sentences for longer ones. This will make the book read more clearly.

To the purists who may be saddened by my presumption I offer my condolences, but not my apology.

Queen of the Haunted Dell

'Mid woodland bowers, grassy dell,
  By an enchanted murmuring stream,
Dwelt pretty blue-eyed Betsy Bell,
  Sweetly thrilled with love's young dream.

Life was like the magic spell,
  That guides a laughing stream,
Sunbeams glimmering on her fell,
  Kissed by lunar's silvery gleam.

But elfin phantoms cursed the dell,
  And sylvan witches all unseen,
As our tale will truly tell,
  Wielded sceptre o'er the queen.

From *An Authenticated History of the Famous Bell Witch*
by M. V. Ingram

CHAPTER ONE

When the terrifying Bell Witch first entered the lives of John Bell and his family in 1817, Robertson County was still a wilderness. Memories of Indian raids were *still* vivid in residents' minds. New settlers *still* raised log cabins. Families *still* made most of what they needed because stores were few. Even Thomas Kilgore, the first settler in Robertson County, was *still* alive. (He would live to the ripe old age of 108.)

Some remnants of that raw frontier are still visible in Robertson County, although most of the original log cabins—including John Bell's—have crumbled away to dust. The area surrounding the town of Adams is rolling farmland—low hills sprinkled with thick forests. Robertson County is both aging and ageless.

Everywhere you look you see abandoned farmhouses. Some are tucked away in deep woods. Some stand sentinel in fields. Some are within spitting distance of Highway 41.

These are landmarks of the past. They are not restored, but are allowed to remain as aging, gentle reminders of life long ago. Memories of the Bell Witch, however, also remnants of Robertson County's infancy, still haunt some of the county's residents today.

Beneath the ground, mysterious limestone caverns snake through Robertson County like a honeycomb. Limestone is laid down in layers called "beds." Beds are created by pressure and the cementing together of small particles of minerals. Falling rain dissolves carbon dioxide in the air, forming carbonic acid. This acid is weak, but it effectively dissolves calcite, the main mineral component of limestone.

When a portion of limestone is dissolved, it creates a "sinkhole." Rain water flows into the sinkhole—then flows horizontally underground, dissolving rock as it goes. Over thousands of years the flowing water forms a cavern.

Stalactites and stalagmites are formed by dripping water rich in calcite and are built up over the eons. Each drip deposits a minute particle, and the formation builds up with each succeeding drip, until a giant stone "icicle" hangs from the ceiling or projects from the floor.

Over 150 caverns, including the infamous Bell Witch Cave, have been surveyed in Robertson County. Countless others wait to be discovered. Caverns continue to be formed by running water. Some believe this subterranean activity is responsible for most of the mysterious incidents above ground.

Running water is intrinsic to Robertson County. Red River forms the northern boundary of Adams. The main road, Highway 41, dips through a man-made gash in the limestone hillside and dips suddenly into the tiny Red River Valley. Red River was once much wider and deeper than it is today. Various flood control and power generating projects have lowered the water level—the TVA at work.

This waterway was once navigable to flatboats all the way to Adams. But the main shipping and receiving point was Port Royal, a few miles downstream. Beyond that spread the mighty Mississippi, meandering down half a continent to New

Orleans. In the 1990s only recreational rafts and canoes traverse the once important Red River.

But in spite of the inevitable changes brought on by time, it is not unreasonable to assume that the witch would still recognize her old stomping grounds if she were ever to return. Enough familiar landmarks remain and, of course, the hills are eternal.

But what if the witch never left Robertson County in the first place, like some folks think....

The Bell Witch once identified herself as the spirit of an Indian whose grave had been disturbed. Certainly Robertson County was no stranger to Indians. And there was certainly plenty for the Indian to be upset about. To whites, real estate was a valuable commodity. To the Indians, land's only value was spiritual.

The Cherokee, Choctaw, and Chickasaw tribes used Tennessee country as a hunting ground. They were there long before the whites infiltrated. Before them were the Mississippian Indians—the great mound builders.

Mounds were built by Indians for various reasons, mainly to bury the dead. They were built by workers who carried endless loads of dirt on their backs. While some mounds were small, others were the size of small mountains.

Not only were the remains of the deceased buried in the mounds, but so were his worldly possessions—weapons, tools, jewelry, pottery, etc. The most famous mound in Tennessee is the one on which the State Capitol is built. Robertson County also has its share of mounds—though they are smaller—some of which have been archeologically explored.

The mound builders became extinct long before white men moved to Robertson County. The Cherokee Indians, on the other hand, were a matter of concern for settlers.

After the English won the French and Indian War in 1763, George III of England, in a fit of charity, declared that the

Appalachian Mountains would form the western boundary for white settlement. Everything west was to be Indian land. Unfortunately, no one paid any attention to "Crazy George," and white settlers poured through mountain passes looking for free real estate. They raised their cabins when and where the notion struck them.

Indians had never been averse to allowing whites to settle on their land. They used Tennessee land only as a hunting ground. Most of their permanent settlements were located to the southeast, on the Little Tennessee River. But the Indians never intended to give their land away permanently. As far as they were concerned, it was not theirs to give but was a gift from the Great Spirit.

When the whites failed to return the land to the Indians, some became angry and tried to reclaim it by force. In spite of their chiefs' best peacekeeping efforts, isolated bands raided up and down the frontier, killing settlers and kidnapping their women and children.

The Indian war began on July 20, 1776, when Cherokee war parties attacked the entire white frontier from southern Virginia to northern Georgia. An angry Continental Congress placed a bounty of 75 pounds for each Indian scalp, no matter who its original owner—man, woman, or child. Armed white forces moved south, burning villages and destroying crops. The Cherokee were eventually forced to sue for peace.

The peace treaty between Indians and whites was signed on June 20, 1777. During the negotiations, three men were brought together—James Robertson, John Donelson, and Richard Henderson. Their idea was to take a group of settlers to an area known as French Lick on the banks of the Cumberland River, about 200 miles east of the Mississippi.

In 1778 Robertson and a group of eight men, including a Negro slave, made the initial trip. When they arrived, they planted corn. Then Robertson returned to the Watauga settlement, in present-day Carter County, Tennessee, and recruited families to make the trip to French Lick.

Robertson and his party reached French Lick on Christmas Day, 1779. Donelson, bringing women and children by boat, arrived April 24, 1780.

Afterward, an influx of settlers arrived at French Lick, and by summer's end there were probably more than 350 persons scattered up and down the Cumberland River. A fort was built as protection from the Indians and was called Nashboro. In 1783 Nashboro became Nashville.

Thirty miles to the north a stockaded fort, Kilgore's Station, had been standing about eight months when Robertson's party arrived at the Cumberland. The fort was built by Thomas Kilgore and was located on the banks of Red River, about three-quarters of a mile west of Cross Plains. This too was an area ripe for settlement.

The government of North Carolina (Tennessee was not yet a state) provided that anyone could secure a section of land (640 acres) if he settled on it and provided proof he was actually farming. In 1778 Kilgore set out to obtain his fair share.

Traveling afoot, Kilgore guided himself by the sun and the North Star. He carried little more than salt and a few grains of seed corn.

When he reached Bledsoe's Lick, he found a colony of about eight families. Those settlers seemed to be making it all right. He enjoyed their hospitality for a few days, then continued his journey west.

Twenty-five miles farther on he found a cave where he figured he would be safe from Indians. It was an ideal hideout. A swift river ran from the mouth and spilled into the middle fork of Red River. Kilgore could walk from the river to his cave, in the shallow water, without leaving telltale footprints.

Kilgore planted his corn and waited for the crop to mature, then traveled back east to prove his claim to the land he had farmed. In the spring of the next year Kilgore returned to Red River, bringing with him a few families who wanted to relocate on the new land.

Foremost of the Cherokee war chiefs was Dragging Canoe, a dangerous, obstinate fellow whose distaste for white settlers was exceeded only by his disgust at his own tribe's feeble efforts to placate them. While Attakullakulla and other chiefs drafted reams of treaties, which would eventually be broken, Dragging Canoe and his followers fumed and plotted.

Finally the dissident Cherokee broke off from the overhill towns and formed the Chickamauga nation. White-hating Creeks to the south, also fed up with their own leaders, joined the Chickamauga warriors for an all-out war against the settlers.

The whites greatly outnumbered the Indians, and Dragging Canoe realized it was folly to attack the older, stronger settlements along the Watauga, Holston, and Nolichucky rivers. He decided to attack the younger settlements along the Cumberland.

On April 2, 1780, Dragging Canoe and his forces tried to raid Nashboro but were routed. Dragging Canoe was determined to carry on his vendetta against the whites, however, and some of his warriors traveled north toward Red River and attacked homesteads.

The Indians raided up and down the frontier. A small colony located near Port Royal was nearly obliterated. Settlers Samuel Martin and Isaac Johnson were captured, but Johnson escaped and returned to Kilgore's Station.

Other miraculous escapes were few. To even venture into the woods to hunt food was to take one's life in one's hands. It seemed like there was an Indian lurking behind every tree, ready, willing, and able to kill yet another white settler and add another scalp to his growing collection.

Indians continued their relentless attacks, and settlers were killed. Red River country was getting more uncomfortable for settlement. Finally, in desperation, Kilgore's Station was abandoned and the settlers joined the defenders at Nashboro. When they finally returned to their homesteads in 1783, the settlers had been reinforced with weapons and additional men.

Indian attacks continued off and on for the next decade, but the whites were better able to fend them off. Then, in 1792, 60-year-old Dragging Canoe dropped dead after a frenzied all-night war dance. His sudden death took much of the wind out of Chickamaugan sails.

Chief John Watts was requested by the Council to replace Dragging Canoe as War Chief. In spite of the fact he was a half blood, Watts's loyalties were totally with the Chickamaugans. For the next two years he continued raids against settlers—from Watauga to Red River.

Then, for some reason, Watts did a total about-face. Instead of fighting, he sued for peace, and on November 7-8, 1794, a treaty was signed.

Two years later Tennessee became a state.

Tennessee County was divided. One part was named Montgomery County. The other was named Robertson County in honor of James Robertson.

In 1788 a family named Fort established a settlement on the north side of Red River, near the present town of Adams. Farmers had instantly recognized this land as excellent for raising tobacco.

Within the next decade a number of families established farms along Red River. They included John and James Johnson, Thomas and James Gunn, Corban Hall, Jesse Gardner, Isaac Menees, Jeremiah and Benjamin Batts, and John Bell. The land was good. The farms grew and prospered.

If one could have met John Bell before the haunting began, it would have been hard to imagine that he, his family, and his home were soon to be visited by a spirit that would not only upset their lives, but the lives of those in the surrounding countryside as well.

Born in Halifax County, North Carolina, in 1750, John Bell was descended from a long line of Scotsmen extending back several centuries. He not only inherited some of their peculiar social traits, but probably absorbed a good measure of Scottish folklore as well. I think he was extremely vulnerable to the paranormal because of a heritage in which the supernatural played an intrinsic part—in much the same way that a Haitian peasant might be susceptible to the influence of voodoo.

John's father, William, no doubt told his son stories passed on by his father before him. In the Old Country unearthly creatures were conjured up and blamed for events for which man had no explanation.

The Scots sometimes explained despotic behavior by saying the perpetrator was in league with the devil. Oliver Cromwell, for instance, was a faithful and true servant of Satan in the eyes of most Scots. After all, wasn't it a known fact that the Puritan ruler did, indeed, consult astrologers—an act clearly at odds with his professed dogma?

A popular topic of conversation around Scottish hearths was the devil and the doings of his evil minions on earth. Women—especially aged and eccentric women—were often regarded as witches.

According to John Aston, the devil became "absolutely familiar on this earth" around the sixteenth century. His tactics had obviously changed from earlier times. Instead of trying to seduce the saints and other just men of God, he concentrated instead on tempting secular folk. And this he did with a vengeance! It seemed for a time like witches were coming out of the woodwork! Even to eighteenth century Scots who had immigrated to America, memories of Janet Bowman (burned in 1572), Bessie Dunlop (burned in 1576), Alison Pierson (burned in 1588), and the evil doings of Dame Fowlis, second wife of the chief of the clan Monro, were still fresh in the storytelling tradition.

William Bell must have told his son John some of these tales around the fireplace at night. Storytelling was a favorite form of recreation in frontier America. There was very little else to do when the day's work was done.

John Bell's ancestors probably arrived in New England in the 1700s, during the great Scottish migration, and moved southward to North Carolina. When he was a young boy, John was apprenticed as a barrel maker, but he became a farmer instead.

In Edgecombe County, Bell met Lucy Williams, daughter of John and Mourning Williams. Lucy's father held vast land holdings west of Tarboro. The couple was married sometime before 1792 (in 1782, according to Charles Bailey Bell, when Lucy was about 12 years old).

No one knows for sure why the Bells decided to pull up stakes and move from North Carolina to Tennessee. Whatever the reason, in 1804, when Bell was 54, he, his wife, and five children arrived in Robertson County and settled 1,000 acres of land on the edge of the Barren Plains, seven miles east of Port Royal, on Red River.

Bell erected a double, one and one-half story log cabin for his family, cabins for his slaves, and various outbuildings.

He would farm there peacefully for over a dozen years, father three more children, and grow prosperous. But in 1817 his contentment came to an end. Thirteen years after arriving at Red River, the infamous Kate came to call. After that, neither the Bell family nor Robertson County was the same again.

CHAPTER TWO

There is a modern-day superstition among young people in Robertson County: If you look into a mirror late at night and recite over and over again how much you hate the Bell Witch, her face will appear in the glass. Apparently Kate doesn't like to be mocked. I interviewed at least two adults who swear up and down that they conjured up the witch when they were children. And they remember the experience as something they would never want to repeat.

One person told me she tried the experiment in her bedroom when she was about ten. Her little pet dog was with her at the time. Her parents had already gone to sleep when she stepped in front of her mirror and began repeating over and over, "Bell Witch, Bell Witch, how I hate you! Bell Witch, Bell Witch, how I hate you."

She continued the chant for three or four minutes, but nothing happened. "Rats," she declared. "I *knew* she wouldn't show up. There ain't no such thing as the Bell Witch!"

Suddenly the little girl felt a chill zip through her like a knife. Then she glanced back at her reflection just in time to see the face of a very old woman leering over her shoulder. She was wrinkled like an old sheet and had a very long nose. Her eyes shone like fire. Her grinning mouth looked like a slash in a ripe watermelon.

The little girl nearly jumped out of her skin. She quickly turned around. No one else was in the room, but the chill remained. She looked back into the mirror. The image was gone. Suddenly she heard a desperate scratching and pawing at her door. Her terror-stricken dog was trying to claw his way out of the room!

Considerably shaken by the vision and by the dog's erratic behavior, she swore she would never try to summon the Bell Witch again. And like so many other Robertson Countians, she became thoroughly convinced the Bell Witch was still lurking in the vicinity and horribly active—just like she was 177 years ago when the nightmare began.

Red River is not a very deep stream these days, and certainly not a useful waterway for river transport. Indeed, only the largest rivers are used to transport goods in the '90s. And on only a few large rivers, like the Mississippi or the Ohio, is this kind of riverboating economically feasible. On these rivers, present-day gigantic steel barges carry hundreds of tons of cargo.

Although the vessels have changed and grown in size over the years, the original principle remains the same. A modern river barge is nothing more than a glorified flatboat. In John Bell's time, flatboats were made of logs; and anyone with enough gumption, and a profitable cargo to ship, could construct one with free materials readily available in the forest.

In 1817 Red River was deep enough to allow flatboats to travel between its banks. In fact, in the early part of the nineteenth century, the Red was a major waterway in North Central Tennessee. The primary point of departure was the bustling Port Royal, located about seven miles west of Adams Station (as Adams was known then).

After serving with Andrew Jackson at the Battle of New Orleans, John Bell, Jr., his brother Drewry, and a friend, Alexander Porter, decided to flatboat a load of Robertson County produce to New Orleans. Their cargo was smoked meats, lard, maple syrup, flour, and tobacco.

The route would take them down Red River to the Cumberland. They would enter the Ohio River at Smithland, a tiny settlement containing about a half dozen log cabins. At the point where the Ohio poured into the Mississippi, a short distance farther, was a large eddy that deposited a vast mud bank on the Illinois shore. The eddy was a menace and had to be negotiated carefully.

The journey would be great adventure for three young men just starting out in life. The 600-mile trip from Cairo to New Orleans was fraught with danger and excitement. Their main problem, other than navigational worries, was river pirates.

At Plum Point, about 100 miles below New Madrid, they would run into one such danger zone. At Plum Point was a line of sandbars, or "bugbears," that literally bristled with sawyers. A "sawyer" is a large tree that falls into the river and floats downstream until it snags a sandbar, causing a bottleneck to river traffic. A sawyer was also a good spot for pirates to lurk. While the flatboat captain labored to clear a path for his boat, he could easily be set upon by pirates. These river scum showed no quarter. They could be counted on not only to rob the flatboat, but also to kill the men sailing her.

Another danger zone on the Mississippi was Montgomery's Point, about 175 miles below Chickasaw Bluffs, about four miles from where White River pours into the Mississippi. That side of the river was said to be infested with robbers, murderers, gamblers, and horse thieves. A prudent flatboat captain would always pass by Montgomery's Point on the opposite side of the river.

All this John Jr. already knew because, like his father, he was a practical man. He never undertook any task without careful planning. He had probably talked to people who had traveled the Mississippi before, and he would profit from their experience. Not only that, but he was a big man in a time when average height was five-foot-six or -seven. John Jr. was six-foot-three and weighed about 190 pounds. Any river pirate would think twice before tangling with him.

At New Orleans, the trio sold their produce and their flatboat as well. Then they returned home to Adams Station over land. Returning with their flatboat upriver, against the strong current, would be more trouble than it was worth. They could easily build another flatboat if they wanted to make a second trip.

If John Bell, Sr., was worried about his 22-year-old son taking this trip to New Orleans, he probably never let anyone know. He, like many of his contemporaries, thought a man should take care of his own business and not burden anyone else with problems or concerns.

John Bell was a rangy man with a long face, a big nose, jug ears, and a stern mouth. His arms and legs were hard with long and stringy muscles. His personality was shaped by a lifetime of practical, as well as ecclesiastical, thinking. He forever dwelt on agricultural and financial matters, not to mention his community image. And, like others of his time, he was perpetually concerned with the eventual fate of his everlasting soul.

Bell had pulled himself up by the bootstraps. He had arrived in Robertson County 13 years before, purchased 1,000 acres of land along the Red River, and had turned his farm into a thriving enterprise. After years of backbreaking work, he could be called a gentleman farmer.

He owned about a dozen slaves, who did the "scut" work; and his four young, strapping sons were old enough to oversee the farm. He no longer had to be in the fields all the time. And that was good. At age 67 he was getting a bit too long in the tooth to work as he had, even a decade before.

Bell was very conscious of his place in the community and proud of the respectability he was able to command from friends and neighbors. In other words, John Bell would do nothing that would make him appear foolish in the eyes of others. And that included making any claim that his house was haunted.

About a year and a half after John Jr. returned from his trip to New Orleans, John Bell, Sr., was walking on the north section of his land with a loaded rifle cradled in his arm. Perhaps he might be able to shoot some fresh game for supper. What he saw, however, was not a rabbit or a deer. Instead he saw something that looked like a dog, but not like any dog he had ever seen before. Certainly it was not one of his animals.

In the days before animal rights laws, stray dogs were fair game for target shooters. So Bell took aim and fired. When the smoke cleared away, the dog had disappeared.

About the same time, his daughter Betsy and son Drewry were strolling through the family orchard when they spied a strange woman walking beside them. Betsy opened her mouth to speak to her, but the woman disappeared into thin air.

That night, strange sounds echoed through the Bell house. They would continue, increasing in intensity, for a year—knocking on doors and windows, sounds of wings flapping against the roof, and vicious sounds of animals fighting. Years later, Richard Williams Bell, who was about five when the disturbances began, wrote about those early days of the Bell Witch infestation:

> This kind of noise continued night after night and week after week. All our investigations were in vain. The

room was overhauled several times, everything moved and carefully examined, with the same result. Finally, when we would search for a rat in our room, the same noise would appear in sister Elizabeth's chamber, disturbing her, and arousing all the family.

And so it continued, going from room to room, stopping when we were all up, and commencing again as soon as we returned to bed. It was so annoying that no one could sleep.

The noise was, after a while, accompanied by a scratching sound like a dog clawing on the floor. Then it increased in force until it became evidently too strong for a rat. Then every room in the house was torn up, the furniture, beds, and clothing carefully examined, and still nothing irregular could be found. Nor was there any hole or crevice by which a rat could enter, and nothing was accomplished beyond the increase of our confusion and evil forebodings.

The demonstrations continued to increase. And finally the bed coverings commenced slipping off at the foot of the beds as if gradually drawn by someone. Occasionally there was a noise like the smacking of lips, then a gulping sound like someone choking or strangling, while the vicious gnawing at the bedpost continued.

There was no such thing as sleep to be thought of until the noise ceased, which was generally between one and three o'clock in the morning.

John Bell first thought the disturbances were caused by earthquakes. He probably remembered the violent shaking in 1811 when the New Madrid Fault on the Mississippi River slipped and caused one of the strongest earthquakes ever felt in the United States. It was so powerful that even the winding course of the mighty Mississippi was changed and Reelfoot Lake was created. The loss of life and property damage was low because the affected land was sparsely populated—only Indians and a few settlers lived there.

Two hundred miles away the shock was felt strongly at Adams Station. But most people did not recognize the shaking as an earthquake. Most thought the trembling was a direct result of the wrath of God punishing a sinful world.

That attitude was typical in light of the religious revival sweeping America at the time—a strong conviction that the world was about as evil as it could get and that God could no longer tolerate its sins without direct hands-on intervention. The earthquake urged Christians to pray harder for divine intervention and a new awakening of religion in the country.

This was a time when, in order to be saved, a person was required to subscribe to a tripartite theology of repentance, faith, and regeneration. Those who did not could expect swift retribution, not only from God but from their peers.

This was a time when moral judgment was not considered the sole province of God. Nearly everyone passed judgment on his neighbor, and if an ill befell someone it was because he had sinned and was a recipient of divine retribution. Even when stories began filtering in from the west, telling what had *really happened* along the Mississippi, diehard revivalists continued to insist that God had made it happen because of the sins of the world.

John Bell, although a Primitive Baptist, probably subscribed to a similar Calvinist theology. After all, hadn't many Scots joined a Baptist church because no Presbyterian church was available? At any rate, Bell was no angel. He was a hard-nosed businessman who turned a profit whenever he could. He had been accused by his own church of usury in a slave deal with a local planter, Benjamin Batts and his wife, Kate. The church had acquitted him of the charge, but the State of Tennessee had proven itself not so openminded.

In August 1817, Bell was convicted on the same charge

The Bell house was a one and one-half story log cabin that, over the four-year haunting by the witch, hosted hundreds—perhaps even thousands—of visitors. After John Bell's death in 1820, Lucy Bell continued to live in the house until her death about 15 years later. The house was then abandoned and used to store grain and for other farm uses until it was finally torn down. (Illustration from *An Authenticated History of the Famous Bell Witch* by M. V. Ingram, 1894)

by a jury in Robertson County Circuit Court. The conviction of an elder of the Red River Baptist Church caused the church's hierarchy to reconsider their own decision. In January 1818, John Bell was expelled.

When it came to religious dogma, even the strongest man cringed during the Revival. Perhaps a similar fault line ran under Red River and that, too, was slipping. Maybe God was going to "get" John Bell for his sins. However, discrete inquiry around the neighborhood soon proved no one else was experiencing noise problems—at least, not at first.

When his earthquake theory failed to pan out, John Bell began to think that vandals were up to mischief, trying to harass the family. All attempts to catch the culprits failed. Meanwhile the noises increased in intensity and frequency—at times so intense that they literally shook Bell's sturdy log house.

Oftentimes the noises seemed to center around Betsy Bell, and the association surely must have caught John Bell's attention. Betsy was about 12 years old at the time the disturbances began. Was she, indeed, the source of the noises?

We now know that poltergeist activity often occurs when a prepubescent is present. "Poltergeist" is a German word meaning "noisy" or "mischievous" spirit. The disturbances at the Bell house certainly fit this definition, and young Betsy was certainly present during most of it.

Charles Bailey Bell, who interviewed his great aunt Betsy during her last years, wrote that when she was away from home the noises continued. He added that the noises sometimes followed her.

At any rate, John Bell was one to keep his business to himself—especially since he was now somewhat of an outcast. Perhaps he was even bitter toward his neighbors. He mentioned nothing of the disturbances to any of his friends and forbade the rest of his family to speak of them either. Bell was not going to appear the fool if subsequent investigation proved them to be of natural origin. But there is no doubt that as time progressed, John Bell's nerves—as well as those of the rest of his family—were slowly becoming unraveled.

About a year after the noises began, John Bell developed a nervous condition affecting his tongue and jaw muscles, which caused him difficulty in chewing and swallowing. When his doctor's cures failed, Bell thought the illness might be caused by whatever godless thing was in the house. For the first time, he broke his silence and appealed to a friend, James Johnson, for help.

There is no way of knowing what reaction Johnson might have had or what he might have initially thought of John Bell when the latter related the events of the previous year. Johnson's first thought must have either been that Bell's ecclesiastical difficulties had caused him to go round the bend or that *the devil's work was truly afoot* in Robertson County.

Nevertheless, Johnson and his wife agreed to spend the night at the Bell house to experience the disturbances for themselves. After supper, Johnson read from the Bible, then prayed long and loud for the Bells' deliverance from whatever might be in the house. Then he and his wife retired to a room next to Betsy's. Neither the duo nor anyone else got much sleep that night.

The house was rocked by heavy pounding. There was gnawing, scratching, knocking on the wall, the sound of overturning chairs, a sound like someone sucking air through his teeth, and the sound of smacking lips—all familiar sounds to the Bell family. Then the covers were ripped from the Johnsons' bed.

A flustered James Johnson sat up in bed and tried to speak to the entity. "In the name of the Lord, what or who are you? What do you want? Why are you here?"

There was a moment of silence. Then the noises resumed, this time with a vengeance. Again the entity pulled the covers from the bed despite the fact that Johnson—who was no weakling—was holding on to them with all his strength. Right then and there Johnson decided that there was no natural explanation for what was going on in the Bell house.

Next morning at breakfast he told John Bell that something ungodly was loose in the house. Furthermore, he said, the spirit was intelligent—able to think for itself. Johnson advised his friend to ask other friends for help. Perhaps, together, they could discover the source of the haunting.

Of course John Bell was reluctant to spread word of his troubles any further than his friend. But he also respected Johnson's advice and decided, reluctantly, to follow his friend's counsel.

John Bell selected his allies with the care one would use to choose the executor of a will. Apparently he chose the right people. Charles Bailey Bell said the select circle stuck with him until the bitter end.

Each night they gathered in the Bell home and listened for the noises and other disturbances. They were never disappointed. Presently a new wrinkle was added to the haunting. The spirit found a voice.

The first intelligible sound from the spirit, other than hysterical laughing, was a repeating of the prayer James Johnson had offered that first night in the Bell house—and in Johnson's own voice! Apparently the witch was quite taken with Johnson's theological eloquence, because after that night she referred to him affectionately as "Old Sugar Lips."

From the first time she opened her mouth the witch never shut it again. She liked to argue theology with all comers. The Rev. Sugg Fort, pastor of the Red River Baptist Church, where John Bell had been an elder, was a frequent combatant. But no preacher in the vicinity, not even the eloquent Mr. Fort, ever had a ghost of a chance in a debate against her.

No preacher or congregation was safe, either, when it came to the witch's scrutiny. One mistake in a sermon, one misquote of Scripture, would result in a severe dressing down.

The spirit attended church regularly, and proved it by repeating the sermons, the prayers, and even the hymns word for word. It made no bones if it disagreed with a sermon.

The witch also noticed errant behavior of churchgoers. One time the witch snitched on two brothers who fell asleep before the final "Amen." She spread that tidbit of gossip far and wide, much to the embarrassment of the offenders. After that episode, churchgoers made darned sure they stayed awake until the benediction.

Like any community, there were also a number of people who were erratic churchgoers. Instead they either worked at some pressing chore or lazed about, fishing Red River. The witch also reported this behavior to the preacher and congregation of the church they attended.

When the witch found a voice she also found an audience. It was inevitable that word of the haunting would transcend the select circle of friends John Bell had chosen to help him. Everybody in the neighborhood, and beyond, wanted to experience the witch—just as long as they didn't have to do it in their own homes.

The witch loved the attention. She also took immense delight in the shock value of some of the things she said. Kate had no peer as a busybody. She kept track of all the doings in the neighborhood. And she happily reported every event in lurid detail.

The situation yielded an unexpected, positive result in Robertson County. When members of the community realized their personal lives were being scrutinized by an unseen entity, they immediately became paragons of Christian behavior.

Richard Williams Bell recalled years later:

This warlock was indeed a great tattler and made mischief in the community. Nothing of moment occurred in the country, or in any family, that was not reported by the witch.

The development of this characteristic led the people to inquire after the news and converse with the witch as they would a person, very often inquiring what was transpiring at a certain place or house in the neighborhood. Sometimes the answer would be, "I don't know. Wait a minute and I will go and see." And in less than five minutes it would report, and the report was generally verified.

Charles Bailey Bell wrote, "It was quite true that it kept all actions of the neighborhood well known, whether good or bad. If a man came home drunk, all the neighbors knew it. If he scolded his wife or whipped the children, it was told. Soon such behavior became unknown in the neighborhood."

As soon as it was possible to talk to the witch, efforts were made to determine her identity. In answering, the witch would beat around the bush. At one time she would give one answer. At other times, she would give another.

One day the witch stated, "I am a spirit who was once very happy. But I have been disturbed and made unhappy."

The spirit was then asked, "How were you disturbed and made unhappy?"

The spirit replied, "I am the spirit of a person who was buried in the woods nearby. The grave has been disturbed, my bones disinterred and scattered, and one of my teeth was lost under this house. I am here looking for that tooth."

Certain activity in the neighborhood would back up the spirit's claim—that is, if it was telling the truth. There were many Indian relics buried about, and one of the favorite recreations in the neighborhood was retrieving artifacts.

Farmers clearing and plowing land occasionally unearthed ancient Indian burial sites. Then the sites were looted of relics. If bones were found, they were scattered. Since the mound builders buried world possessions with the body, these burial sites were rich with pottery, jewelry, arrowheads, and tools.

Richard Williams Bell said that before the haunting began, a neighborhood youth, Corban Hall, had found such a burial site. He picked up a human jawbone and brought it to the house. While sitting in the hallway, he threw the jawbone against the opposite wall. The blow jarred loose a tooth, which fell through a crack in the floor. Young Corban's thoughtlessness had angered John Bell, and he insisted that the youth return the bone to the site where he had found it.

Is it possible that this event contributed to the haunting of the Bell house by the witch? Was the witch actually the ghost of the Indian whose grave Corban had disturbed and whose tooth was lost forever beneath the Bell house? (John Bell tore up the floor of his house and searched for the tooth but found nothing.)

Another time the witch answered, "I am the spirit of an early immigrant who brought a large sum of money. I buried my treasure for safekeeping until needed. In the meantime I died without divulging the secret. I have returned in the spirit for the purpose of making known the hiding place. I want Betsy Bell to have the money."

This answer, of course, alerted all the treasure hunters in the neighborhood. The spirit said the money was buried "under a large flat rock at the mouth of the spring on the northwest corner of the farm, on Red River." Her description was so precise that no one could mistake the place.

Drewry Bell, Bennett Porter, and James Johnson set out the next day to seek the witch's treasure. They found the stone easily, but it was huge and much work was required to remove it. Then they began to dig.

Several sweaty hours later, they had opened a hole about six feet square by six feet deep. All that the perspiring, angry men found at the bottom was more dirt and rock. They looked at each other with disgust on their faces. They had been had! That night the spirit had a great hoorah and gleefully chided the men for being so gullible as to believe her.

The witch had shown a wide playful streak. But a darker side would soon manifest itself—a sinister character that showed all too graphically that in addition to playfulness, she was also capable of physical abuse and murder!

CHAPTER THREE

The witch had made it clear from the very beginning that she was out to get John Bell—even if it meant killing him. Bell fell seriously ill at the end of the first year of the haunting. He suffered from a disorder that affected chewing and swallowing. Even then he suspected that whatever was causing the disturbances in the house was at the bottom of his physical ills. A short time later, when the witch found her voice, his worst suspicions were confirmed.

Whenever Bell's name was mentioned in the presence of the witch, she erupted with a volley of verbal fire against him—calling him every vile name in the book. (On occasion, the witch could cuss like a sailor.) Her voice would rise to a nerve-racking pitch.

Periodically Bell was seized by body contortions and facial twitching which lasted one or two days. This, of course, interfered with working and caused him to take to his bed. And all the time he lay there, the witch raved and ranted around the house, yelling at Bell and hurling vile curses in his direction—giving him little peace.

Other times Bell would suddenly slap wildly at his body,

yelling and screaming that a thousand pins were sticking him. Then, as suddenly as the pain had begun, it would end.

Bell and his doctor, George Hopson of Port Royal, were helpless to combat the malady. Throughout the haunting, Bell's afflictions became more frequent and progressively worse. The witch declared to all that she, and she alone, was the cause of his troubles. She said she was bound and determined to get John Bell any way she could. Yet not one time did the witch mention a single specific reason why she had it in for the Bell family patriarch. Nor did there seem any clear-cut reason why the Bell house was singled out for the haunting. But some believed the Bell problem was caused by a local eccentric, Kate Batts.

The trouble began when John Bell and Kate Batts entered into a business deal that turned sour. As stated before, Bell had sold Batts a slave and had charged her excessive interest.

Kate Batts was a portly woman and a faithful churchgoer who liked to use bombastic language because she thought it made her appear better educated than she was. Kate Batts's husband was an invalid. So she took care of most of the family business and household accounts. Although not as prosperous as the Bells, the Battses had a good farm and owned a small number of slaves.

When the Bell/Batts business deal soured, Kate Batts spent a great deal of time maligning Bell's character. According to local legend, Kate Batts confronted Bell and said, "Oh yes, old John Bell, you have your broad acres and your comfortable home. The future may look bright to you now. But just wait and see what sad changes are soon coming to you and a certain member of your family."

Of course Bell dismissed the curse as the ravings of a crazy old woman. Even as the disturbances began in the Bell household, no one seemed to remember the old woman's curse. Then one night, when the witch was talking to a number of visitors in the Bell house, the Rev. James Gunn asked her who she was.

"Brother Gunn, I believe you are a good man and I will not tell you a lie," the spirit answered. "I am Kate Batts's witch."

This startling revelation brought an expected round of gasps, but Gunn remained undaunted—at least on the surface. Maybe he was finally getting to the bottom of the mysterious Bell haunting.

"How do I know what you tell me is true?" Gunn asked the spirit.

"You just watch her pretty close and you will see and hear her do many things that will convince you that she is a witch," the spirit replied. "She begs every woman she meets to give her a brass pin. And when she gets as many as she wants, she puts them on a stump in John Bell's woods and tells me to use them. Haven't you seen that old long-legged devil writhe and twist and say that something was sticking pins all over him?"

Indeed Gunn had!

Reports of this conversation soon spread over the neighborhood. Certain elements in Robertson County began to shun Kate Batts, either in fear of what she *might do to them* if they invoked her displeasure or in sympathy to John Bell. Most took the spirit's advice and began watching Kate Batts's behavior very closely, especially when strange things began to happen.

Churning butter was an exhaustive but necessary chore for many a frontier housewife. Milk was poured into a wooden bucket, then sloshed back and forth with a paddle on the end of a pole until the butter was finally separated from the liquid.

One woman, a close neighbor of Kate Batts's, was busily churning and churning, but still no butter appeared. Exhausted and sweating, she thought about old Kate and the terrible things she was supposed to be doing to John Bell. Maybe she was putting the whammy on her neighbors as well.

The frustrated churner finally declared, "I verily believe old Kate Batts has bewitched this milk and I'm going to burn her out!" And with that, she plunged a red-hot poker into the milk, then sat the churn aside.

A short time later the same neighbor had occasion to visit the Batts home, located across a field from where she lived. There she found Mrs. Batts sitting in a corner nursing a severely burned hand. She had mistakenly picked up the wrong end of a red-hot poker!

Kate Batts's behavior was unusual in other ways. She had an old gray mare that she used exclusively for riding. The fly in the buttermilk was that *nobody had ever seen Kate Batts ride.* In spite of this she had her slaves saddle the horse every morning. Then when she had to go somewhere, she walked beside the saddled horse with two young slave boys on either side and her waiting maid, Phyllis, leading the mare.

Sister Batts, a devoted churchgoer, was a charter member of Red River Baptist Church. She was one of the first worshippers to attend when it opened its doors in 1796. Invariably late for services, she would arrive just in time to work herself up into a spiritual frenzy before the final "Amen."

She also attended the revivals that were so popular at the beginning of the nineteenth century. One time Red River Baptist Church hosted a revival presided over by Rev. Thomas Felts. Felts was a hellfire-and-brimstone preacher who could whip a congregation into a frenzy in no time at all. As such, he was extremely popular with the faithful because they felt he was in the Spirit.

This particular revival had been going full steam for several days. One night, Felts had preached a particularly rousing sermon. He had finished and the congregation was just launching into a hymn when Kate Batts and her entourage walked through the door. It didn't take long for her cup to overflow with glory.

Down on all fours beside the mourning bench was Joe Edwards, fervently praying for forgiveness of past sins. Edwards, like most other people in Robertson County, was neither all good nor all bad. But like everyone else who attended Felts's revivals, fervent preaching had had an enormous effect on his conscience.

Harriet Parks Miller wrote that the entire congregation had surrounded Edwards and was urging him on. Sister Kate, however, did them one better. She rushed up to where Edwards was kneeling, spread her copper-colored riding skirt over him, and sat down. Since she weighed over 200 pounds, Edwards thought he "was in the last throes of the struggle with sin and that the devil was on top."

"Oh Lord, I am sinking!" the tortured man screamed. "Take my burden, Jesus, and make Satan turn me loose, or I will go down and be eternally lost. Oh save me, blessed Lord."

Seeing that it wasn't the devil at all, but the portly bottom of Sister Kate sitting atop the poor man and "driving him down," some members of the congregation invited her to take a more traditional seat on one of the pews. Sister Kate replied with her customary fusillade of misused 50-cent words:

"No thank you. This is so consoling to my disposition that I feel amply corrugated. I'm a very plain woman, and do love to homigate near the altar when the Lord is making confugation among the sinners."

"But Sister Batts," pleaded the frustrated deacon, "you're suffocating the mourner!"

"Yes, bless Jesus. Let him suffocate. He's getting closer to the Lord."

Suddenly Edwards could no longer take the weight bearing down on top of him. His arms and legs began to give way.

Two members of the congregation caught Sister Batts just in time before she landed on the floor. Edwards rose, his eyes rolling, and began shouting for his deliverance. Sister Batts joined him:

"Bless the Lord. Bless my soul. Jesus is so good to devolve His poor creatures from the consternation of Satan's mighty dexterity!"

By this time, it was all the congregation could do to contain their mirth. Rev. Felts, seeing that the situation was about to get out of hand, uttered a quick benediction and dismissed the congregation. As they filed from Red River Baptist Church, a loud, collective laughter was heard throughout the countryside.

A great deal of folklore has sprung up concerning John Bell and his relationship with Kate Batts. One very odd legend accuses Bell of murdering Mrs. Batts.

Supposedly old John Bell locked her up in the smokehouse and starved her to death. Some say that is why the spirit infested the Bell house and caused him so much grief. It was actually the ghost of Kate Batts wreaking vengeance.

This story, of course, is ridiculous. Kate Batts was alive and well all though the haunting—and for some years after as well.

We can only wonder, too, if John Bell really cheated this eccentric, excitable woman. According to Charles Bailey Bell, his great-grandfather was practically a saint with money to lend.

In *The Bell Witch: A Mysterious Spirit*, he wrote of John Bell: "He was always generous in making loans to his neighbors, taking no mortgages and letting them have such amounts as they wished, which they invariably paid back."

But yet it is an established fact that in 1817 Bell was convicted by a Robertson County jury of usury in a slave deal with Benjamin Batts. If he, indeed, was guilty, Kate Batts certainly had reason to hate old John Bell. But whether she actually conjured up a "witch" to torture him and his family is another thing altogether.

If the spirit had targeted only Bell, that would have been one thing. Unfortunately, others were also singled out for abuse. His daughter Betsy is a prime example. What did Kate Batts have against a 12-year-old girl? And what about Joshua Gardner? Had she also had problems with Joshua's father? Unfortunately the answers to these questions are unanswerable—lost forever in time.

Pretty, blue-eyed Betsy Bell holds a unique place in the annals of parapsychology. She was the brave young woman who bore much of the brunt of the physical torture doled out by the infamous Bell Witch of Tennessee.

She was slapped, struck, and pinched on numerous occasions by the entity. The large red welts that appeared on her face and body bore mute testimony to the abuse she suffered—the senseless attacks that nearly drove the young woman mad. Her cheeks would turn red from repeated smackings, and her hair was pulled with such force that she would scream in agony.

Not only did the witch physically abuse Betsy, she tried to ruin the girl's life as well, interfering with her romance with a local boy, Joshua Gardner. The witch had a foul mouth and told stories in public about Betsy and Joshua— whether true or not. Joshua, at least on the surface, ignored the witch's ravings as being that of a maniacal demon. He loved Betsy too much to give a hang what the witch said.

But Betsy believed that if she continued her romance with Joshua, both might find themselves in grave danger from the witch. The mere mention of Joshua Gardner's name would prompt the witch to fly into another rage and begin attacking Betsy again.

The witch made Betsy's life miserable wherever she went.

Pretty, blue-eyed Betsy Bell received the lion's share of abuse from the witch. The invisible creature slapped her with such force that red welts appeared on her face. The witch also caused Betsy to enter trance-like states in which she appeared to be dead. And, finally, the witch wrecked her romance with Joshua Gardner, forcing the pair to go their separate ways. This illustration is based on the facial characteristics of Bell descendants living in the last part of the nineteenth century and may be a very accurate likeness of "The Queen of the Haunted Dell." (Illustration from *An Authenticated History of the Famous Bell Witch* by M. V. Ingram, 1894)

When it seemed as if Betsy could take no more abuse at home, her family would send her to a neighbor's house for the night.

Her first night away from home was spent with her best friend, Theny Thorn. The early part of the evening went swimmingly. After eating supper and talking for a while, she and Theny retired for the night. No sooner were they in bed than they heard a loud knocking on the bedroom door.

Then the door appeared to fly open and a strong blast of wind hit both girls squarely in the face. The candle went out. The bed quilts were jerked off.

Theny jumped out of bed to close the door but found it was already shut—it had never opened at all! Then Betsy felt a soft hand pat her on the cheek, and a voice said, "Betsy, you should not have come here. You know I can follow you anywhere. Now get a good night's sleep."

Understandably it took Betsy and Theny a long time to fall asleep that night. The girls kept anticipating the witch's next move. Fortunately they were not disturbed further.

After Betsy returned home, her mother said the witch had told her everything that had happened at the Thorns' home. Kate had told Lucy not to be alarmed. Betsy was safe and would be home the next day.

When the Bell Witch first came to call, she acted very much like a poltergeist. A number of people in the neighborhood believed Betsy to be at the bottom of the disturbances. But as the haunting progressed, it became clear that, in addition to being an expert trickster, Betsy would also have had to practice ventriloquism. At first the witch was mute and restricted to rapping, pounding, and incoherent mumbling. Later on it would be difficult to imagine that any human being—much less a 12-year-old girl—could make the same kind of noises (and with the same volume) that the witch did.

In addition to all her other problems with the witch, Betsy also suffered fainting spells. She experienced shortness of breath, sensations of being smothered, and panting. She became exhausted and lay as if dead, losing her breath for as much as a minute between gasps while unconscious. The spells lasted 30 to 40 minutes and then passed, leaving her as if nothing had happened.

Visiting Betsy Bell was an adventure. One day some of the young people in the neighborhood decided to have a sleigh-riding party at the Bell house. They got more than they bargained for.

In those days farmers made heavy slides to haul tobacco from the fields. Constructed of wood, they had a pair of runners and a plank floor built on top. Tobacco leaves would be piled high on a slide, and a team of horses pulled it to the barn for curing. In winter, young people liked to hitch horses to these slides and use them as sleds for joyriding around the countryside.

After dinner the girls piled on a large slide sitting by the front door while the boys went to fetch the horses. Suddenly the witch's voice rang out: "Hold tight when we get to the corner!" At the same moment, the sleigh took off without benefit of the horses and raced around the house.

The girls screamed and tried not to be thrown off. After three rounds, the sleigh stopped at its point of departure, right in front of the astonished boys. After the excitement died down, the boys hitched up the horses and the young people took a "normal" sleigh ride.

As news of the Bell Witch spread, the house was filled nightly with friends and supporters of the family, as well as the curious. It is said that John Bell, Sr., never turned away anyone. He spent his money to keep his guests fed. He offered them his bed. Privacy was out the window. There were few times when the family was truly alone.

Those who didn't come to the Bell home for just a show wanted to help rid the family of the witch. Some thought they could outsmart the witch. Others believed they could defeat the spirit with brute strength.

One of John Jr.'s best friends was Frank Miles. He was a powerful man, standing well over six feet tall and weighing at least 250 pounds—every ounce muscle. His strength was legendary, and he was said to be the most powerful man in Robertson County.

Miles came to see himself as protector of the Bell family, especially Betsy Bell. Miles hated the witch and longed to get his powerful hands around her neck and throttle her. But, of course, this was not possible. One does not simply catch a spirit and choke the life out of it. But that didn't stop Miles from trying. He spent many nights at the Bell house trying to do just that.

In return, the witch taunted him unmercifully. She dared him to catch her. Miles would be lying in bed, and suddenly the covers would be jerked from him. Sometimes Miles caught them in mid flight. Then he would try with all his might to prevent the covers from being pulled off completely.

Unfortunately, the witch's physical powers were considerable and no match for any human—not even Frank Miles. If Miles did manage to grab the covers, the room would echo with the sound of ripping fabric. Then Miles would find himself sitting upright in bed with shreds of Lucy Bell's handmade quilts clutched in his powerful hands.

Miles was not a man of even temperament, and the witch capitalized on this weakness. Whenever she was making his life miserable, the witch would cackle. Then she would shout that he was certainly a strong man but his strength meant nothing to her. Miles would get red in the face and storm around the room, vainly clutching at thin air, trying to get a grip on his nemesis. Even after failure piled on failure, the determined Miles never gave up.

Frank Miles, shown here in later life, was said to be the most physically powerful man in Robertson County. But in every contest of strength, he was easily bested by the witch. A man with a violent temper, Miles wished he could get his hands around the witch's throat and throttle her. (Illustration from *An Authenticated History of the Famous Bell Witch* by M. V. Ingram, 1894)

The witch taunted Miles further by abusing Betsy in his presence. He could hear the blows being delivered, see Betsy reel from the invisible force, and watch helplessly as angry, red welts appeared on her face. But he could do nothing.

Miles was obviously a simple man who did not understand that he was bringing some of the attacks onto Betsy himself. He would say to her, "Sit by me, little sister. Nothing will bother you while I am here."

This infuriated the witch, who would yell at the top of her voice, "Go home! You can do no good here!" Then, as if to underline Miles's helplessness, the witch would pull Betsy's hair and pinch her cheeks with such fury that the girl would scream for mercy. Miles would rage around the room, stomping on the floor and daring the witch to assume a shape that he could get hold of.

One time during one of these shouting matches, the witch started slapping Miles himself. Like Betsy, Miles recoiled from the hard blows while the spirit demanded he leave the house before she knocked his block off. Of course, this made Miles even madder, more frustrated, and more determined to catch the witch in solid form to return the favor.

He called the witch a coward for picking on Betsy and refusing to confront him. Eventually, however, it dawned on Miles that he was making things worse for Betsy by fighting the witch. So he stopped and directed his attention to Betsy and offered her all the sympathy he could muster.

The witch was also violent with others. In later life, Betsy Bell told Charles Bailey Bell that she, Frank Miles, and her father were not the only ones the witch abused. Her brother Drewry also received his share of knocks from the unseen entity. Guests, too, received their lumps from the witch.

"I have seen big, strong men jump from their chairs and yell in pain, becoming so frightened that they had to be helped out of the house," Betsy recalled. "It was not imagination on their part, as the blows were heard and spots were seen on their faces where they had been struck."

If the witch took pleasure in abusing John Bell and his daughter Betsy, she took an even greater pleasure in overwhelming Bell's wife, Lucy, with kindness. Lucy Bell, according to the witch, was the "most perfect woman to ever walk the face of the earth." The witch kept her informed of all the doings in the neighborhood and offered her advice on domestic matters that always seemed to pan out. The witch also kept Lucy Bell in touch with the activities of her relatives who were still living in North Carolina.

Whenever Lucy invited neighbors to her home for Bible study or quilting, the witch was in attendance. She provided fresh fruit during refreshment time—where she got them from no one knew. Most were tropical, nearly unknown in frontier Robertson County.

Where the Bell Witch was concerned, there seemed to always be a direct correlation between behavior and treatment. Lucy appeared, at least on the surface, tolerant of the witch. This was the case even when the entity was abusing her husband and daughter. Some people believed that Lucy Bell, herself, was the real power behind the witch—that she exercised control over the entity.

Richard Williams Bell wrote, "These neighbors who knew the family so well and believed Mrs. Bell to be such a good woman, also believed Betsy to be good and esteemed John Bell just as highly. These neighbors thought if it were a spirit from hell, as many believed it really was, such a spirit could have been controlled by a greater spirit. Mrs. Bell could have been endowed by her Creator with a spirit and soul that the cruel visitor had neither the power nor disposition to worry."

Be that as it may, Lucy Bell followed a policy of placating the witch, and the entity responded in kind. Apparently the witch was easily bamboozled by kindness. Jesse Bell's wife, Martha (whom the witch called "Potts"), noticed her mother-in-law's successful policy of humoring the witch. Martha, in turn, listened patiently to the witch's prattle and did not incur her wrath.

Lucy Bell liked music and, by all accounts, the witch could sing like an angel. She frequently asked Lucy if she wanted to hear something. Lucy would reply, "Yes. Sing something sweet."

When Lucy was under the weather, the witch often sang to her. As was the custom in Robertson County, and on the rest of the frontier, friends would visit the sick and watch over the sickbed—attending and comforting. At these gatherings in the Bell house, the witch sometimes turned up and asked Lucy if music would help her feel better. Lucy invariably said yes. Then the witch would begin singing in a beautiful, unearthly voice.

As the witch sang, tears would roll down Lucy's cheek like a river. Neighbors attending Lucy would turn away to hide their own weeping—whether it was because of the sweetness of the witch's song or in sympathy for the torment of the Bell family.

At any rate, when the song ended, Lucy always remembered her manners and complimented the witch. "Thank you," she would say. "That was so sweet and beautiful. It makes me feel better." The witch was so susceptible to flattery from Lucy that she was like putty in her hands.

On one occasion Lucy Bell fell critically ill. Although the doctor was hopeful she would recover, others were not as optimistic.

On the Tennessee frontier, any serious illness could easily result in death. There was little medicine available, with the exception of home remedies. Surgery was almost unknown.

People saw tragedy every day. They lived with it like a member of the immediate family. They knew it as well as the backs of their hands. Death was accepted philosophically—

the will of God. The average life span then was hardly 40 years. Death was even more probable for children. Couples conceived large families because they knew they might lose up to half their children to disease and accidents.

Pioneers were well-acquainted with the telltale signs of impending death—the wasting away of the flesh, the transparent look of the skin, the sickly-sweet odor surrounding the deathbed. In the last stages of a terminal illness, the patients often became delirious. They would lie in bed and unconsciously pick at the bedclothes with their fingers. The last sign was the surest indication of all. Unfortunately, Lucy had reached this stage.

John Bell was beside himself with worry. Neighbors called in Preacher Fort to pray. This he did with customary fervor. The doctor continued pouring medicines down Lucy's throat without appreciable improvement. Everyone was gathered around the bed, waiting for Lucy to breathe her last.

The witch, however, was optimistic. She thought that her precious Lucy would recover if provided with foods more agreeable to her appetite. So the witch said to Lucy, "Hold out your hands, Luce. I will give you something."

Lucy did as she was told, and a large amount of hazelnuts appeared out of thin air over her bed and dropped into her outstretched hands. She complained that she was much too sick to crack the nuts so she could eat them. Then the ever-accommodating witch provided her with grapes, showering them onto her as before—out of thin air.

After that day, Lucy's condition improved. In a week she was well enough to get out of bed. And soon she was fully recovered.

John Bell, Jr., was another member of the family that the witch treated with respect. Perhaps it was because he took no guff from the entity and often told her, in no uncertain terms, what he thought of her. He had many conversations with the witch and once asked her why there was such a difference between her kind treatment of his mother and the punishment doled out to his father and sister. And the witch's answer to the question, as told by John Jr. himself, was quite revealing.

John Jr. dared the witch to inflict the same kind of punishment on him that she did his sister and father. He called the witch a coward and declared he was not afraid of her. "Your actions could not give pleasure to the devil himself," he shouted.

"John," the witch replied calmly, "I admit it's beyond my knowledge why I don't punish you for what you say to me. Somehow your daring me to do as I like to you, no matter what, gives me respect for you. I will not favor you by punishing you instead of Betsy. I know you and I am convinced that you'd like it for me to change her punishment to you.

"There are reasons why I will not punish you both. There are many things I want to say to a human being with enough intelligence to understand. Even though you think of me as a monster doomed to inhabit your world, I still like to talk to a soul who is not so frightened, nor has so little sense, that he could not understand the things I say.

"You're quite right. I'm not happy in your world. I have never been happy here. The day that I could have been happy passed hundreds of years ago.

"John, don't you think when such a being does anything at all which you might call good, no matter how insignificant, that a human being who is of the spirit that the Creator of all things wishes, would feel more kindly toward that being? Your mother is such a human.

"She is protected from all wickedness by her goodness and gentleness toward all creatures. She is always appreciative of the smallest gift or tribute, even when it is offered by a demon."

John Jr. wrinkled his forehead and said, "The only virtue

I've known you to have other than kindness to my mother is that you do not deny being just as mean as you are. Sometimes I think you are here simply because you could not get along with your fellow demons. They threw you out!"

The witch neither denied nor admitted this to be the case. Instead she said, "I must remind you of another of my virtues. With you and Old Luce I have been absolutely truthful. I will never tell you or your mother a lie.

"You may not understand all I say to you. But remember, John, it will be true. Things I have told others, which were lies, were not important. I told them to prove how foolish the average human really is. The man who is easiest to be shown a fool is always ready to display his lack of sense over and over again. I'm sure you'll agree that a demon is not the only being who laughs at the foolish things men do and encourages them to continue their foolish acts."

If this were truly the case, as the witch had stated to John Jr., *then the entity was really an outcast demon*, and, as such, probably possessed greater powers than any ghost, or even witch. Certainly she was more intelligent than either. And as the infestation of the Bell house continued, her presence grew even stronger.

More and more, word of the strange goings-on at John Bell's house spread. Newspapers printed accounts of the happenings, and it seemed as if everyone in America wanted to experience the haunting.

Fools and geniuses, adventurers and quiet folk, politicians and common people arrived at John Bell's door in droves. Bell seldom turned anyone away.

It went without saying that even the famous would eventually appear to see for themselves the famous haunting. So it was just a matter of time until the greatest swashbuckler in Tennessee, yea even in America, would eventually come to call.

CHAPTER FOUR

As a frontier lawyer and judge, Andrew Jackson had seen more than his share of unruly characters loitering in the American backwoods. The land west of the Alleghenies was wide-open to settlement and attracted thieves and cutthroats as well as decent folk trying to make a new start. But nothing Jackson ever encountered—either personally or professionally—ever compared with the infamous Bell Witch.

One day the hero of New Orleans and a party of friends visited the witch. Jackson was so unnerved by the experience that, on his return to Nashville, he remarked to all who would listen, "I'd rather fight the entire British army than to deal with this torment they call the Bell Witch!"

Jackson was born on March 15, 1767, the son of Andrew and Elizabeth Hutchinson Jackson, a poor farm couple who had emigrated from Northern Ireland in 1765. Raising the child became the sole responsibility of his mother. Unfortunately the father had died a few days before his son's birth.

Being on his own almost from the start, young Jackson grew up tough—a product of the American frontier. His mother had hoped he would be a minister, but young Jackson was interested in more exciting pursuits—horse racing, cockfights, and high adventure. However, she was able to insure that her son received a good education.

In a day when newspapers were rare—even if there were people who could read them—Jackson became the town "reader." Several times a day he would stand in a public place and read the latest news aloud to the crowd. In 1776, at age nine, Jackson read a copy of the newly adopted Declaration of Independence to his neighbors in Waxhaw.

Jackson served in the Revolutionary War in South Carolina's mounted militia, joining in 1780 at age 13. He was captured by a British raiding party a year later and was badly treated by his captors.

One time the British commander wanted his boots cleaned and ordered the 14-year-old Jackson to the task. Jackson refused. In a fury, the officer lashed out at Jackson with his sword, cutting the boy's hand to the bone and wounding him in the head. Then he forced Andrew and his brother Robert to march 40 miles to a military prison.

In prison the brothers caught smallpox. Robert died of the disease, but young Andrew survived. Eventually he was released in a prisoner exchange, arranged by his mother.

The smallpox and the British commander's sword left more than just physical scars on the young adventurer. There were emotional scars, as well. Then and there Jackson began his lifelong dislike for the British.

After the war, Jackson studied the law with Spruce McCay in Salisbury, North Carolina, and was admitted to the bar in 1787. In 1788 he moved to Tennessee. He first settled in Jonesborough. Barely a year later, he landed in Nashville. Soon after, he was appointed Attorney General.

Jackson had his work cut out for him. Too many of the earliest settlers of Nashville—rugged individualists all—refused to pay their debts, or, if sued, ignored the law altogether. The no-nonsense Jackson threw many of them into

Andrew Jackson—soldier, Indian fighter, jurist, and President of the United States—once said he would rather fight the whole British army than deal with the Bell Witch. (Illustration from *Life of Andrew Jackson, Vol. II* by James Parton, 1870)

prison.

In 1796, Jackson was elected the first member of the U.S. House of Representatives from Tennessee. The following year, he was named to serve in the Senate. He took a leave of absence from his duties in 1798, returning home to Tennessee. He found that he liked Nashville much better than Philadelphia, so he resigned his Senate seat. Shortly thereafter, the Tennessee Legislature elected him a Justice of the State Supreme Court.

Then, in 1801, Andrew Jackson was made a major general in the Tennessee militia. An influential enemy, former Governor John Sevier, had vehemently opposed the appointment. But a supporter, then Governor Archibald Roane, ignored the old Indian fighter's earnest protest. Sevier's objection was based on his opinion that Jackson was little more than a barbarian and an unfit leader of men.

Perhaps Sevier had a right to complain. Jackson was known far and wide for his volatile temper. This particular facet of his personality involved him in a number of duels. But he managed to kill only one man in this gentleman's version of revenge. Charles Dickinson had accused Jackson of being a coward and a scoundrel. Furthermore, he had made insulting remarks directed at Mrs. Jackson, the former Rachel Donelson. This was too much for the general, who in 1806 called Dickinson onto the field of honor.

In 1813—during the second war with the British—Tennessee Governor Willie Blount ordered Jackson and his men to reinforce American troops at New Orleans. But the expedition turned out to be a wild-goose chase. No sooner did Jackson and his men arrive in New Orleans, spoiling for a fight, than he was told to disband his army. Jackson was fit to be tied. The government had failed to provide food, transportation, medicine, or even pay for his men. So he refused to demobilize, and marched his army, intact, back to Tennessee.

After the muddle in New Orleans, Jackson took command of 2,000 men in a campaign against the Creek Indians in the South. They fought a battle near the Creek village on Horseshoe Bend on the Tallapoosa River on March 27, 1814. Before he nearly wiped out an entire Indian force of 800 braves, Jackson gallantly allowed women and children to cross the river to safety. As a result of this battle, the Creeks surrendered 23 million acres of land to Georgia and Alabama.

Once again Jackson and his men took off for New Orleans. This time it was their job to thwart an expected British attack on the city.

When his army arrived on December 2, Jackson found the city in great disorder. Although weak with dysentery, Jackson proclaimed martial law and began setting up the city's defenses. He even enlisted the help of Jean Laffite and his Caribbean pirates to help defend the city.

On January 8, 1815, the British attacked at dawn with 8,000 men. They suffered a terrible defeat—300 men killed, 1,250 wounded, and 50 captured. Of the defenders, only 14 were killed, 39 wounded, and 18 captured.

One of Jackson's aides at New Orleans was John Bell, Jr. When, a few years later, word reached Jackson that his friend's family was being harassed and tortured by an invisible creature from hell, the general naturally felt obliged to investigate.

Jackson knew there had been an enormous amount of visitors to the Bell house. Not knowing how many people might be present during his visit, and not wanting to impose on Bell's hospitality, Jackson and his party decided to bring their own provisions and camping gear. The general had set aside a week for his visit.

It was late in the afternoon when Jackson and his party of horsemen, accompanied by a covered wagon drawn by a team of four horses, slowly made their way up the turnpike toward the Bell house. A few hundred yards from the front door someone in the group made a disparaging remark about the witch. Suddenly the wagon stopped—the horses were unable to pull it any farther.

They were on level ground. The wagon driver yelled and cursed and snapped his whip, but to no avail. The horses pulled and strained, pulled and strained. They reared and snorted and bellowed. They jerked the hitch against the metal straps and threatened to tear the wagon tongue out by the roots. But the wheels still would not turn. Finally, in frustration, Jackson's party stopped, the horses snorting and heaving.

Jackson dismounted and examined the wagon. He declared there was no reason why the horses could not pull it. So the driver climbed back into the boot, snapped his whip, and urged the horses onward.

Once again the four powerful horses pulled and jerked and pulled and jerked. Still they were unable to move the wagon.

Suddenly General Jackson shouted, "It is the witch!"

From the roadside came a disembodied voice: "They can go now, General."

No one was in sight. But the entire party had distinctly heard the voice—a woman's voice calling out to the general. Then it spoke again and promised it would see all of them again that night.

A short time later the group arrived at the Bell house and began unloading the wagon. John Bell, himself, came outside to greet them. Since Jackson was not the usual curiosity seeker, but a distinguished guest, Bell invited all to come into the house. After eating dinner, while waiting for something to happen, they sat around the parlor talking about the Indians who had lived on the farm.

In Jackson's party was a man who fancied himself a "witch tamer." Whether he actually believed he could control the supernatural or he believed the Bell haunting was the product of sheer fakery is uncertain. But he declared to all that no witch would appear while he was there.

Other members of the party appeared to humor him. They said that, indeed, no witch had ever appeared in his presence. The witch tamer declared he had the witch bluffed. He was carrying a pistol loaded with a silver bullet and said he had an itchy trigger finger.

Jackson was clearly showing his impatience that nothing had yet happened. He wanted to see if his witch tamer carried any clout.

After several hours of silence from the witch, the frustrated witch tamer stood up and dared the witch to come out. Suddenly he leaped from his chair, grabbed the seat of his pants, and screamed, "Boys, I'm being stuck by a thousand pins."

The disembodied voice of the witch cried out, "I am in front of you. Shoot!"

The witch tamer drew his pistol and took a bead on the thin air in front of him. He tried to shoot, but the gun would not fire. Then the voice cried out mockingly, "It's my night for fun!"

Suddenly the man was assaulted by unseen hands. Everyone present heard the repeated slapping of the man's jaws and saw him recoil from the invisible blows. Then his hands shot to his face.

"It's pulling my nose off!" he screamed.

The witch tamer shook free and made a break for the front door, which flew open of its own accord. The man shot through it like a bullet, running for all he was worth toward the wagon, yelling all the way. The voice followed him, offering all sorts of advice on how to be a witch tamer.

Jackson roared with laughter and told John Bell that he had never seen anything so funny in his entire life.

A few minutes later, inside the house, the disembodied

voice spoke again: "There is another fraud in your party, General. I'll get him tomorrow night. It's getting late. Go to bed."

The other men in Jackson's party looked nervously at each other and refused to spend the night in the house. They asked the general if he didn't have some sort of pressing business in Nashville. But Jackson was fascinated. He wanted to know the identity of the other fraud in his party and how the witch was going to expose him.

The whole group slept in their tents that night in spite of John Bell's gracious invitation to sleep in soft, warm beds. In the end, Jackson's men must have convinced the general that it was in their best interest to go home with all dispatch. By noon the following day, the entire party was in Springfield, 12 miles from the Bell farm.

None ever returned.

Mostly the witch was heard and not seen. But on a few occasions she was said to have appeared in solid form. The old woman Betsy and Drewry saw strolling in the orchard on the first day of the haunting, for example, might have been the witch. And there were some other occasions where she possibly materialized in some form or another.

One time Betsy and some children were visiting a nearby woods to gather flowers for Easter Sunday. A short time later she returned home without a single blossom—and nearly frightened to death. She told her mother the following story:

"As I reached overhead to break off dogwood boughs for the children, a voice spoke. 'Betsy Bell. Don't break a flower. If you do you will pay well for it.'

"I looked and 20 feet from me, across a wagon road running through the woods I saw, as distinctly as I see you, a ghostly looking woman. She was dressed in pale green and suspended from the limb of a large red oak tree. She was holding on with both hands and her frail figure swayed in midair.

"I turned away. But when I looked the second time it was the same.

"I hastened home with the children, all the while watching them closely to see if they noticed anything unusual—but they did not. They wondered why I did not get the flowers we went for. I did not tell them the real reason."

Another time Richard Williams Bell, Joshua Gardner, Alex Gooch, Betsy Bell, and Theny Thorn decided to have a bit of sport by allowing the dogs to chase rabbits around the countryside. After being turned loose, it didn't take long for the excited animals to flush a long-eared varmint out of the bushes.

The dogs chased the rabbit across the field, the young people in hot pursuit. Then the rabbit began running in circles, from the top of a nearby hill down to the bottom, then back again—four or five times. The young people followed the yapping dogs as best they could, trying to cut the rabbit off.

During the chase, Betsy couldn't help but wonder why the rabbit didn't try to duck under a bush or leap down the nearest hole. That would have been its nature. But this rabbit's behavior was different. It was almost like the animal knew exactly what it was doing—consciously trying to tire its pursuers. Had it not been that she knew better, Betsy would have said the rabbit was actually enjoying the chase!

One by one, the exhausted dogs dropped out of the sport while the young people dropped to the grass. Seeing its pursuers scattered on the meadow, out of breath, the rabbit paused for a moment. Then it scampered out of sight.

That night the spirit said, "Josh can sure run like a dog. I almost had to dodge between his legs. The rabbit you were chasing was me."

That remark—that he could run like a dog—was perhaps the nicest thing the witch would ever say about Joshua Gardner. Like all the other people she harassed, the witch offered no explanation for her intense dislike of Gardner. She hated him and that was that! The witch also spent a great deal of time pleading with Betsy Bell to end her relationship with him.

If the Bell Witch disliked Joshua Gardener, the feeling was certainly mutual. Gardner, unlike most of the neighborhood, was privy to the details of the haunting almost from the very beginning. Like Frank Miles, he saw himself a protector of the family—especially of Betsy. Joshua tried to solve the haunting, but the witch frustrated his every attempt.

Joshua was in love with Betsy Bell, a condition that had existed for years. Both were pupils at a log schoolhouse presided over by Professor Richard Powell, a subscription schoolteacher, well-known in the neighborhood as "The Bachelor Teacher."

Both Betsy and Joshua had entered Powell's school at age ten. Betsy stayed under Powell's tutelage until she was 14. Her innocent charms were not lost on Professor Powell, who was about 25 years old at the time. But the difference in their ages, of course, prevented him from following his heart. She was still attending his school when the witch first appeared at the Bell house.

Joshua Gardner had tried everything in his power to discover the nature of the Bell Witch—and, hopefully, to discover her weakness. His first personal encounter in the Bell house began one night around midnight. He was sleeping upstairs in one of the bedrooms when he felt something begin to pull the covers from his bed.

Joshua raised up and grabbed the end of the quilt and tried to prevent its moving. But, as usual, it would take a stronger man than he to do it.

With John Bell's permission, Joshua invited Frank Miles to spend the night with him in the same room. Miles, of course, was thought to be the strongest man in Robertson County. It was said he could crack a large black walnut

Joshua Gardner courted Betsy Bell for many years, over the witch's
vigorous objections, and the pair even became engaged. But Betsy
feared the witch would make their lives miserable if they ever did
marry. Much to her sorrow, she was forced to break off their engagement in 1821. (Illustration from *An Authenticated History of the
Famous Bell Witch* by M. V. Ingram, 1894)

between his teeth as easily as a normal person could a crack a hazelnut. If anyone could cope with the unseen forces, no matter how powerful, Frank Miles was the man!

Lucy Bell furnished the men with the strongest, thickest quilt she had so they would have something substantial to hold on to. Also, underneath the pillows, the pair was provided with a bolster—a long pillow that extended from one edge of the bed to the other.

About midnight the men felt the covers begin to move, and before they could act, the heavy quilt was snatched from the bed. Then the pillows were removed by unseen hands, as well as the heavy bolster.

Miles's temper exploded and he screamed, "See here Miss Witch, or whatever you be! I'll give you a tussle over this bolster. I'm tired of this one-sided affair."

Then he flung his massive frame across the retreating bolster. It did no good, and the bolster was pulled away and landed on the floor beside the bed, Miles sprawled on top of it. This was the first time that anyone could remember Frank Miles so thoroughly outdone in a test of strength.

As the years went by, young Joshua Gardner couldn't help but notice the physical changes Betsy was experiencing. And it was pretty doggone certain that the increasing attraction between them didn't escape the witch's attention either.

Betsy blossomed from a gangly 12-year-old girl into a beautiful young woman. While Professor Powell kept his silence and nursed his aching heart, Joshua Gardner became an ardent suitor. And the more ardent he became, the more the witch was determined to put a stop to the budding romance.

One afternoon a group of young people was gathered on the front lawn of the Bell house enjoying each other's company and the fine June weather. As usual, Joshua and Betsy soon stole away from the main group and found a secluded spot all to themselves.

They had just settled down under a large pear tree when they heard the witch's voice. At first it was barely audible. Then it seemed to gradually approach them. Soon they could make out the words. "Please, Betsy Bell. Don't marry Joshua Gardner. Please Betsy Bell. Don't marry Joshua Gardner." Then the voice died out in the distance. Those were soon to become familiar words that Joshua and Betsy would hear over and over again in the months to come.

Near Red River is a cave with an entrance so large that a party of picnickers can comfortably seat themselves at the entrance. Like other accessible caves in Robertson County, this one was used to store perishable foods because the temperature inside remained at about 56 degrees year-round.

The cave became known as the Bell Witch Cave because the witch's voice was often heard near it, along the river. There was never any clear-cut indication, however, that it was the witch's home, although many believe that she lived there—and maybe still does.

Located in the center of a large bluff overlooking Red River, the cave's entrance is formed like a long tunnel, extending back at about a 45 degree angle. In wet weather a river of water gushes from its entrance and spills over a 30-foot cliff in a spectacular waterfall. During these times the cave is practically inaccessible, unless a person swims against a 25-mile-per-hour current. However, when the weather is dry the cave beckons to the adventure seeker, in spite of the thick mud that ices its floor like chocolate frosting on a cake.

Like all caves, this one is dangerous. But that only adds to its lure.

Passing through the entrance, the visitor comes upon a large room, draped with colorful stalactites and stalagmites. The second room has a kind of upstairs. From there, the passageway gets smaller and smaller.

One time a group of Betsy's friends was exploring the cave, using candles as their only source of light. One of the boys came to a place that was so small that he had to get on his hands and knees and wiggle though. To his horror he became stuck. His candle went out and others in the party could not find him in the total darkness. He screamed for help, but his echo bounced off the cave walls and seemed to be coming from all directions at once.

Suddenly the boy heard a voice behind him—the voice of the witch. "I'll get you out!" she said. He felt his legs being pulled, and he was dragged through the mud backwards all the way to the entrance. Finally he stood up, coughing and gagging, nearly suffocated by the mud that had been forced down his throat.

Although the witch periodically abused Betsy, she some-times showed her kindness. There was a kind of dichotomy in the witch's behavior towards her.

On one hand, the witch seemed bent on destroying Betsy's personal life with Joshua Gardner. But on the other, she seemed to fall all over herself to make things pleasant for the young girl—especially when Betsy entertained friends at home.

It would almost seem like the witch was trying to protect Betsy from Joshua—even to the point of trying to beat her into submitting to her wishes. As the witch once told John Jr. when he asked her about the treatment of Betsy, future gen-erations would prove her right. At any rate, we'll never know for sure. But visiting Betsy Bell could be a great adventure.

One year John and Lucy Bell threw a birthday party for their daughter. Young people from all over the neighborhood were invited. The witch, of course, was in attendance and took a great interest in the games being played. She also noticed the variety of food on the table and decided she could improve the rations.

Suddenly the witch cried out, "I have a surprise for you. Come and see."

When the young people gathered around the table, they were delighted to see a large basket of colorful, exotic fruits sitting there. "Those came from the West Indies," the witch announced. "I brought them myself. Now eat and be merry."

Some of the fruits she had brought had never been seen in Robertson County before, so there was a mad rush to snatch them up. The witch, obviously pleased with herself, joked, "I would have brought a few bottles of fine wine, too. But I don't think the preachers would have approved. But, of course, those who have the most to say about strong drink likes best to drink it."

And then there was the time that the witch might have even saved Betsy's life. Betsy Bell told the following story:

I'll never forget the horseback ride which Richard Williams [Bell], Rebecca Porter and I took one early summer day. We were all riding beautiful, spirited young horses. We rode to the bend of Red River, on the north side of the farm, where there were magnificent poplar trees of great height. Some were six or eight feet in diameter.

In the river bend were the Indian mounds where we often dug up relics such as arrowheads, tomahawks, etc.

We were caught by a terrible storm after we arrived. The wind bent the trees and carried away the leaves. Now and then limbs were blown off, some falling around us. Before we had left the house the spirit told us not to go, that a storm was coming. However, it had a way of saying that when we were going off (just as our father did when he wanted us to stay home) and told us many things to scare us that were not true.

Just as the storm came up it called to us to cross the river as quickly as possible or some of us would be killed. We were ready to take this advice and quickly started to the river. Limbs and leaves were falling.

The horses decided they would go home and not cross the river. We could do nothing with them. They reared and snorted. They ran sideways, threw up their heads, and plunged. They were entirely unmanageable. We were badly frightened.

A voice called out, "You little fools. Hold tight now and say nothing to the horses."

Suddenly the horses quit rearing and went straight to the river crossing, getting us completely away from the storm, no doubt saving our lives. Afterwards we saw numbers of these immense trees blown up and fallen in every direction along the path we were trying to follow.

By the beginning of the fourth year of the haunting, nearly everyone in Tennessee, Kentucky, and beyond knew about the strange things going on at the Bell residence. In the evening the curious would assemble at the Bell house. In the soft, warm glow of candlelight—kerosene lanterns were virtually unknown at the time—they would sit and chat, waiting for the arrival of the witch and hoping she would have something to say.

When the voice did arrive, which it almost always did, it would seem to come from everywhere at once. After the initial shock of hearing what seemed to be something from another world, the curious would settle down in their chairs and listen to the witch wax eloquent on any subject that struck her fancy or tell in graphic detail of the day's doings in the neighborhood.

Sometimes she would repeat a sermon that she had heard in a local church—word for word—perfectly mimicking the voice of the parson who had delivered it. Other times she would sing, in an incredibly beautiful voice, unknown love songs or hymns which some people said were reaching human ears for the first time. Or she'd entertain the assembled multitude with uncensored, bawdy drinking songs of which she seemed extremely fond.

The witch's interests were eclectic, to say the least.

The witch was also an effective, self-styled disciplinarian, especially when it came to John Bell's slaves, whom she considered lazy. Some former Bell slaves told tales of the witch to Charles Bailey Bell, and he wrote:

Harry, the Negro boy, some eighteen years old, came in the mornings to kindle the fires which were all in open fireplaces. Wood was still being used when members of the Bell family were growing up.

He was late getting in for a few mornings. His Master scolded him and told him he must get in earlier. The very next morning Harry was late again. While he was on his knees trying to blow the coals into a blaze, suddenly pieces of his kindling began beating him all over the body. Finally he was jerked up across a chair and given such a beating that the blows were heard all over the house.

While the beating was being administered Harry let out such yells and begged so for his life that John Bell was alarmed, fearing the Negro would be disabled. It [the witch] then told Harry if he were ever late again, he would be beaten to death and thrown into the fire. Harry was never late again.

After that incident, Harry seemed to be a special target of the witch. Charles Bailey Bell tells another story about Harry and the Bell Witch:

Harry told that one night after carrying in the kindling and wood for the next morning, he was on his way to his cabin when a voice commanded him, "Go right over to Mr. James Johnson's and cut wood and kindling for his morning fires. He and his folks are sick and I told him I would send you. Step right on. James Johnson is the best man in this country. Your Master will be glad I sent you. Don't stop to ask him."

Harry hurried to Mr. Johnson's home, some half mile away. That gentleman told him the spirit had promised to send him to get up the wood, just as it had said, and he felt very thankful that Harry came.

The spirit then asked Mr. Johnson if he wanted Harry to come next morning and kindle his fires and said, "It will be no trouble as Harry just likes to make fires on cold mornings. If you are going to be sick long, Harry will come every day and see to your fires. I'll tell his Master to send him, and you know he will be glad to have it done."

The witch's attitude toward Negroes was probably nothing more than an accurate reflection of the contemporary attitude of slaveholders in the antebellum South. The big difference was that while masters believed a slave's place was in his own cabin, many treated their Negroes as trusted members of the family. The so-called Simon Legrees of the plantation set were few and far between.

On the other hand, the witch hated Negroes, pure and simple. One day Lucy Bell decided to use one of the slaves in a plan to rid her house of the witch.

The witch followed John Bell everywhere he went. If he was on a horse, the witch rode with him. If he was in the fields, the witch was at his side. If Lucy could eradicate the witch from the house, at least, her husband would have some sanctuary. Lucy thought she would capitalize on the witch's distaste for Negroes to accomplish this end.

In the days before running water, folks just didn't bathe as often as we do today. Hard physical work in the fields raised sweat that, in turn, activated bacteria on the skin. By our present social standards, most people of the time would be socially unacceptable to our noses. Slaves had less opportunity to bathe than their masters.

Lucy Bell owned a slave named Anky. Anky was big and buxom, about 18 years old. Lucy reasoned that if Anky took up residence in the Bell house, the witch would be so offended that she would be compelled to leave. Years later, Richard Williams Bell told the story:

Mother had determined to test her plan for getting rid of the witch. She told Anky that she wanted her for a house girl and desired she should sleep in her room. Anky had misgivings. But at the same time she was complimented by the fact that Mother had chosen her.

She asked Mother if she reckoned the witch would pester her. Mother assured her that there wasn't much danger of that. The witch would be too busy entertaining company to take any notice of her.

Anky believed Mother. Mother told her that she should keep the appointment a secret from all the other slaves. No one else, not even members of the Bell family, should know of it. That way, a test would be made as to whether the witch would trouble her or not.

One evening after supper, Anky quietly slipped into the room with her pallet and spread it under Mother's bed. It was a high bedstead with a fringed counterpane hanging to the floor. Underneath it, Anky was hidden completely.

She was delighted. Not a soul except Mother knew she was there. Soon after, the room filled with visitors, keeping up a lively chit-chat while waiting the coming of the witch. Mother joined the group, anxious to see the outcome of her scheme.

The voice of the witch rang out as expected and started screaming, "There is a damn nigger in the house. It's Ank. I smell her under the bed. She's got to get out!"

Suddenly, from underneath the bed, came sounds like a man clearing his throat, hawking and spitting vehemently. Anky came rolling out like a log starting downhill. Her face and head were literally covered with foam-like white spittle.

In spite of her size she sprang to her feet with the agility of an acrobat and started screaming, "Oh, missus. The witch is going to spit me to death!"

Anky ran through the house and flew through the front door, running for all her might back to the slave cabins.

Then the witch said to Mother, "Say, Luce. Did you bring that nigger in here?"

"Yes," Mother confessed. "I told Anky she might go under my bed where she would be out of the way, to hear you talk and sing."

"I thought so," replied the witch. "I guess she heard me all right. Nobody but you, Luce, would have thought of a trick like that. If anybody else had done it, I would have killed the damn nigger."

The witch, at times, acted like both an enlightened philosopher and an extremely cruel child. The occasions when she showed great philosophical insight and common sense were more than nulled by the times she threw tantrums because she didn't get her way.

The witch hated people indiscriminately, though she did seem to respond to kindness, tolerance, or a no-nonsense attitude. Cool heads found the best way to deal with the witch was through placation. Lucy Bell and Martha Bell followed this policy and were left unscathed.

John Bell and Betsy Bell reacted badly to the witch's shenanigans. Betsy became hysterical when the witch abused her. The town bully could not have hoped for a more reactionary victim.

The witch also seemed to enjoy reactions from the living that reinforced her power over others—a power, in part, derived from fear of the unknown. The victim, more likely than not, was chased, physically attacked, or verbally abused, and quickly left the Bell house because of the uncertainty of what the witch would do next.

Then there was John Bell, Jr. He had the witch pegged for the demonic child she was. He refused to allow the witch any power over him—either real or implied. He gained respect from the witch because he sassed her and told her in no uncertain terms what he thought.

When the witch tested the waters to see what she could get away with, John Jr. always brought her up short. He constantly questioned the witch's motives. For example, the witch was well-versed in theology. She claimed to subscribe to the divinity of Jesus Christ. Yet John Jr. constantly reminded the witch of her own hypocrisy. How could any intellect who professed to be aware of goodness and mercy be so cruel in her behavior toward people who had done her no wrong? In answer to his questions, the witch usually embarked on a long, rambling response. The main purpose of this rebuttal seemed bent toward justifying her actions.

Still, John Jr. and the witch had many conversations together, which the former passed on to his son. Not only were the witch's answers to historical and theological questions startling, some of her predictions of the future were to prove uncomfortably accurate.

CHAPTER FIVE

One of the strangest associations any human being has had was the relationship between John Bell, Jr., and the Bell Witch. Charles Bailey Bell wrote, "He knew more than any other person of the spirit, but had less to say about it than anyone."

John Jr. was 24 when the witch first appeared at the Bell home and 28 when she departed the first time. He was 35 when she returned. Charles Bailey Bell added, "When it returned after an absence of seven years, he was at the height of his intellectual powers. During its first visit he was of an age to deliberate over these demonstrations in an intelligent manner. His natural good sense and courage enabled him to form opinions far better than the ordinary person."

John Jr. is an important character in this story, not because of what the witch did to him, but what the witch told him. John Jr. was her "Moses"—a mortal hand-picked to deliver an important message to other mortals. Whatever civilization made of the information was its business, just as long as the message was delivered. The problem was that John Jr. was an unwilling messenger. He remained stubborn and unyielding in his dealings with the witch, and the witch's missive nearly missed being published at all.

John Jr. was born in North Carolina in 1793, several years before his family immigrated to Tennessee. He was a deadeye shot with a Kentucky flintlock. He could hit the head of a turkey at 300 feet and was also an expert in barking squirrels from trees. His prowess with a rifle served him well at the Battle of New Orleans and during the Indian campaigns, both under General Andrew Jackson.

When the haunting began, John Jr. followed his father's directive that details of the "family trouble" not be discussed outside the home. Then, as word of the witch leaked out, John melted into the background, seeming to know instinctively that his interference in the witch's activities would only make matters worse for his father and sister. And through it all he remained virtually silent on the subject of the witch. He didn't even discuss the haunting with members of his own family, unless he was forced to by circumstance. Furthermore, almost no one knew about the clandestine conversations he was having with the witch.

In later life, John Jr. chose to divulge details of the haunting and the witch, including, to the best of his recollection, all the things the witch had said to him. These things he told to his son Dr. Joel T. Bell in a three-day-long marathon interview.

According to Charles Bailey Bell, his father was surprised at John Jr.'s sudden willingness to talk about the witch. Joel had not heard him speak of the haunting but three times in his life.

The son dutifully took down reams of dictation. Then he, in turn, passed the notes on to his own son, Charles Bailey Bell.

"The Spirit talked to [my grandfather] on the important topics of the day," Charles Bailey Bell wrote, "and told of happenings in the past of which no one had ever heard. It prophesied about what was to be expected in the future, much of which has already happened [as of 1934, when Bell's book was published].

"My father knew many people, relatives, and friends who had talked to the Witch, but advised me that the confidential conferences between the Witch and his father were the most amazing experiences to which any human being had ever been subjected. Not only the Bell family, but the whole world would finally be interested."

Had it not been for the fact that John Jr., for some unknown reason, decided to break his long-standing silence and tell his story to his son, no one would have known about the witch's chillingly accurate predictions. The fact that the witch visited for the second time and had long conversations with John Bell, Jr., was unknown to everyone except Frank Miles.

During the witch's first visit, 1817-1821, John Jr. avoided becoming directly involved in the upheaval going on in his parents' home. He enjoyed a kind of diplomatic immunity simply because he refused to take any guff from the witch. He also refused to criticize the witch's behavior in front of others.

Certainly he was present some of the time when the witch physically abused his sister Betsy. On these occasions John Jr. would stand back and observe what was happening. His heart probably broke when Betsy screamed for mercy during the attacks. But John Jr. wisely realized there was nothing he could do. It didn't escape his attention that violent reactions from people like Frank Miles only made the witch behave even worse.

No indeed, John Jr. seemed to instinctively know how to handle the witch. And his behavior towards her yielded unexpected dividends. The witch confided in him.

This was no unintelligent ghost—this infamous Bell Witch.

She had intellect and she had personality. She displayed all the emotions normally assigned to human beings—love, hate, joy, sorrow, prejudice, and an overwhelming desire to command respect. She had both a good and a bad side. Furthermore, she seemed to appreciate John Jr.'s policy of non-interference. Well, at least she respected it. She would meet him in special places and at quiet times when the two could be alone to talk freely about whatever was on their minds.

John Jr. minced no words when it came to voicing his opinion of the witch's brutal behavior toward his sister and father. And the witch had said she could not understand why his sharp words did not cause her *to openly attack him.*

There seemed to exist an uneasy peace between them which provided an avenue for frank discussion. For example, one day John Jr. asked the witch why she acted so vile. He demanded to know, for instance, why the witch was so against the marriage of his sister to Joshua Gardner.

"If she marries Joshua," the witch replied, "she can never have a day of happiness or peace. That is certain. That is the only reason I will give you. If you cannot see that it is a good one, it is because of your stubbornness and not lack of sense. Betsy will take your advice. She knows that you idolize her and that your advice would be the best for her."

John Jr. replied that he could not help but notice the thinly veiled threat that she will never have a happy day if she were to marry Joshua Gardner. Then he asked the witch whether he was to assume that she would make their life miserable if they did marry.

"You may form your own conclusions because I shall not answer that question," the witch answered. "But once and for all, Betsy would do better not to marry him regardless of anything I may do. Future generations will prove it to be so."

One topic that the witch loved to argue was theology. Her arguments were so airtight that even the most eloquent preachers of the day could not compete with her logic. During these discussions the witch never spoke out against Christianity. Rather, she often said that people who failed to recognize the divinity of Jesus Christ would be truly lost.

But John Jr. thought this declaration by the witch hypocrisy. Considering the witch's treatment of his father and sister, not to mention the blasphemous tirades she unleashed on various occasions, he considered the witch a damned liar, and plainly told her so.

"It is useless for you to defend your case to me," he told the witch one day. "I see right through you. Furthermore, I don't believe Jesus Christ appreciates your defense of His divinity. Why should he? You have not influenced, and do not know, the great Christians of the world."

"You are correct in a way," the witch answered. "My influence would not produce great results. I admit that I'm an outcast. But you are quite wrong when you say that I don't know the great Christians of this world.

"I have seen the great things they have done. And I know the minds of some of the world's greatest Christians. Certainly I could not influence them as you said. But I can inform you of what great thinkers conclude.

"Napoleon, for instance, has repeatedly recognized the eternal future as taught by Jesus Christ. When his great friend Marshal Duroc lay dying on the battlefield, he told him they would meet again in another life—that this was not the end. Napoleon has said he wants to die a Christian.

"He now is dying slowly on the rocks of St. Helena. He has no hope of living much longer or escaping. Napoleon has said that his empire was founded by armies and that kingdoms of most of the great rulers of the past have been so founded.

"While he was present soldiers followed him and would cheerfully die at his command. But now that he is done, he no longer has the love of his former followers. His empire is gone and he thought all great earthly rulers had to be present to sustain their kingdoms.

"Jesus Christ would never be forgotten. His kingdom was founded on love, and after centuries it is stronger now than at any time. And this, no doubt, proved to Napoleon that Jesus Christ was God.

"John, do not let the world forget that Napoleon's downfall was caused by forgetting that God's laws were still in force. He thought only of himself. His ambition was unquenchable. Had he stopped at the time which would have been best for France and the whole of Europe, he would have been acting for the everlasting good of mankind.

"Napoleon is mortal. He forgot God until trouble came. Then, like a real man with a soul, he acknowledged the divinity of Jesus Christ. We can clearly see that he repented and will die quietly resigned to that fate, death, to which all human beings must bow.

"The world will never forget Napoleon, but the greatest thing he ever did they will not know of. That was his acknowledgement of the divinity of Jesus Christ. In the end he realized himself only a human and that his downfall was the result of a selfish foundation of his empire by force.

"After the fall of Napoleon, the leading allied powers formed the Holy Alliance, taking the New Testament as their guide. They proposed to rule according to the Christian religion, love and justice being their aspiration.

"If these sovereigns were sincere, the world would be safe. But they are human and looking after their personal political interests, always leaning toward despotism. In time their governments will fall.

"These sovereigns are professing to believe in the Christian religion but are applying it in a way to suit their personal interests. They are not thinking of the welfare of their subjects but really have formed an alliance for sovereigns to hold their subjects under tyrannical subjugation if they wish.

"There is unrest and revolution in Europe. There will be continued dissatisfaction until the final upheaval caused by sovereigns entirely forgetting their professed allegiance to Christianity. They seek only to satisfy their ambition.

"I have witnessed the things I am telling you. I'm sure the final penalty will be terrible.

"In your country, John, you have a president who is earnestly looking after the welfare of his fellow citizens. He desires protection of the United States from European aggression. Before his administration is over his endeavors will place the Americas in a position of security."

This was the first example of a prediction-come-true made by the witch. In 1823, after the witch departed the Bell house for the first time, President James Monroe outlined his support of the independent nations of the western hemisphere against European interference "for the purpose of oppressing them, or controlling in any other manner their destiny." Known as the "Monroe Doctrine," the statement declared the United States would allow no new European colonies to be created in the Americas. It also prevented existing European colonies from extending their boundaries.

"President Monroe is a man of honesty," she continued, "whose administration is giving the people a realization of what may be accomplished rapidly in this country. While not assuming great Christianity, the people are Monroe's first thought, and his actions are that of a Christian.

"Thomas Jefferson's esteem for Monroe's goodness is as great as a man can have for another. Monroe's contact with Jefferson has been of great value to him and the nation.

"You remember Jefferson was the author of the statute of Virginia for religious freedom? Jefferson still lives [he died on July 4, 1824] and you know what he thinks of Christianity."

John Bell, Jr., had a number of these private conversations with the witch. Perhaps he was surprised that the witch could show such insight. He obviously did not know what Napoleon was thinking concerning his immortal soul. He might have known more about James Monroe, but he certainly knew nothing of the Monroe Doctrine. That was still years in the future.

But there were more predictions to come from the witch, and John Jr. would be the recipient. Although he saw few come true during his lifetime, history would prove the witch was no mere "guesser." Before any of this could come to pass, however, the witch had a little unfinished business to take care of—the death of old John Bell.

CHAPTER SIX

Stories about the witch multiplied like a bin full of rabbits. Richard Williams Bell wrote:

The excitement in the country increased as the phenomena developed. The fame of the witch had become widely spread and people came from all quarters to hear the strange and unaccountable voice.

Some were detectives, confident of exposing the mystery. Various opinions were formed and expressed. Some credited its own story and believed it an Indian spirit. Some thought it was an evil spirit. Others declared it witchcraft. And a few unkindly charged that it was magic art and trickery gotten up by the Bell family to draw crowds and make money.

These same people had stayed as long as they wished, enjoyed father's hospitality, and paid not one cent for it, nor did it ever cost any one a half shilling. The house was open to every one that came. Father and mother gave them the best they had, their horses were fed, and no one allowed to go away hungry. Many offered pay and urged father to receive it, insisting that he could not keep up entertaining so many without pay. But he persistently declined remuneration, and not one of the family ever received a cent for entertaining.

Father regarded the phenomena as an affliction—a calamity. Such accusations were very galling, but were endured.

By 1820, hundreds of people from all over had spent time with the Bell family, had wrecked the Bell front yard with their horses and wagons, and had drained most of the Bell fortune when John Bell insisted on feeding and putting up his guests. In the meantime, Bell was suffering more and more at the hands of the witch.

He suffered spells and contortions of the face, twitching and tics, and stiffness of the tongue. The spells lasted one or two days, then he would be up and about his business as usual.

But the witch taunted him at every opportunity. She threatened him with bodily harm, and his spells became more frequent and severe as time passed.

The witch now called John Bell "Old Jack." Every time she spoke to him—or about him—it would be punctuated with curses and oaths. And, as usual, the witch never mentioned any reason for her dislike of John Bell, nor did Bell do anything to incite such hatred.

Early one morning in October 1820, John Bell asked his son Richard to accompany him to the pigsty, located a short distance from the house. He said he needed help in separating the pigs intended for fattening from the stock hogs.

About halfway between the house and the sty, one of Bell's shoes was suddenly jerked from his foot. Richard retrieved the shoe and replaced it on his father's foot, tying the strings in a double knot.

A few steps farther, the other shoe repeated the same performance. Once again, Richard retrieved and replaced the wayward shoe.

A few steps farther and both shoes jerked off. Then Bell received a sharp blow to the face that sent him reeling. Stunned, he sat down on a log to recover. Suddenly his entire face began jerking involuntarily. His shoes, this time tied in double knots with the strings pulled very tightly, flew off his feet again.

Demonic shrieks filled the air, then slowly died away. John Bell's face stopped twitching. He sat on the log for a very long time, breathing heavily. Then he looked at Richard, tears streaming down his face.

"Son, it won't be long before you won't have a father," he said. This horrible thing is killing me by slow torture. I don't think I have much longer to live."

Then he lifted his face to Heaven and began to pray for deliverance from the witch.

After the episode at the pigsty, John Bell's condition worsened. He took to his bed more often. Periods of recovery became more infrequent.

By early December, Bell was greatly weakened by spells. No sooner had he recovered from one onslaught than another laid him low.

On December 19, John Jr. and Drewry were out feeding the stock. When they returned to the house they found their father unconscious. All efforts to rouse him failed. John Jr. sent for Dr. George Hopson. He arrived from Port Royal two hours later. Shortly thereafter John Johnson, Alex Gunn, and Frank Miles arrived.

"What kind of medicine have you been giving him?" Dr. Hopson asked.

John Jr. replied that his father had actually been taking three medicines, and he went to the cupboard to fetch them. When he opened the door he found not the three familiar medicine bottles, but a single container holding a brown liquid.

He picked up the bottle and sniffed the contents. "I've

never seen it before," he said.

Suddenly Frank Miles shouted, "The damned witch did this!"

Roaring with laughter, the witch replied, "He will never get up. I did it."

"Did what?" John Jr. asked.

"I gave it too him!" the witch shouted gleefully. "I gave him a dose from the vial. Now he will die!"

Frank Miles began a swearing tirade that matched anything the witch could deliver. When his vocabulary was exhausted, Miles began to pray like a Methodist in search of redemption. In the meantime the rest of the group tried to coerce the witch into telling them where the vial of brown liquid had come from and what it contained. No one, not even Dr. Hopson, could identify it. But the witch kept her silence.

Then Dr. Hopson suggested the contents of the vial be tested to find out what it contained. Alex Gunn left the house. He returned a few seconds later with a scraggly cat he had caught in the yard. John Jr. dipped a broom straw into the vial of unknown liquid and drew it across the animal's tongue. Then everyone stood back to see what would happen.

The cat suddenly began having convulsions. John Jr. angrily threw the bottle into the fire, and instantly a blue flame shot up the chimney. They looked back at the convulsing cat, but the animal was dead!

John Bell never regained consciousness, nor was he able to swallow the legitimate medicine that Dr. Hopson had brought. All day long, on the 19th, John Bell lay in a stupor. Dr. Hopson said he detected a strange odor on Bell's breath that could have come from the vial. To make matters worse, the witch taunted John Bell the whole time he lay on his deathbed, laughing hysterically and singing derisive songs at the top of her voice.

The next morning, John Bell died. The witch told everybody present at the time that she would attend the funeral.

Then, mysteriously, she stopped talking.

John Bell's funeral was one of the largest ever seen in Robertson County. Hundreds of people attended—some to pay their respects to the old patriarch, but others to see what the witch would do. The latter group was far from disappointed.

The funeral was made a mockery by the gloating witch. Over the newly filled-in grave, the witch cheerfully offered mourners a concert of bawdy drinking songs.

Then Bell's friends and relatives realized there was something else to worry about. Since the main target of the witch's wrath was now dead, what would the spirit do to Betsy?

But after John Bell's funeral, the witch's activities decreased. She was not heard from so often and was not as cruel to Betsy. Throughout the winter of 1821, however, the witch remained in the neighborhood.

Meanwhile, Betsy and Joshua Gardner renewed their relationship and celebrated Easter Sunday by becoming engaged. On Easter Monday three young couples, including Joshua and Betsy, decided to have a picnic at Brown's Ford on Red River. It was a bright, warm day. The weather could not have been more perfect. All thoughts of the witch had vanished.

Joshua and Betsy, picnic hamper in hand, soon reached the Red River Valley. More picnickers arrived. They spread their blankets on the ground and began unpacking food. Some cast lines into Red River in hopes of catching a few fresh fish to bolster the already sumptuous feast spread before them.

Before long Richard Powell, the schoolteacher, appeared. Powell was politicking to become a candidate to represent Robertson County in the Tennessee Legislature. He had heard about the picnic and, since most of the picnickers were former students, decided to drop in.

Powell was still much attracted to Betsy Bell. He had first

Richard Powell was a subscription schoolteacher who first taught
Betsy Bell when she was ten years old. Over the years, Powell saw
her emerge into a fine young woman. Although he was considerably
older that Betsy, he fell in love with her. After the witch broke up
the romance between Betsy and Joshua Gardner, Powell stepped in
and courted Betsy, finally marrying her. (Illustration from *An Authenticated History of the Famous Bell Witch* by M. V. Ingram, 1894)

taught her when she was about ten years old and had seen her grow into a fine young woman. Now he had heard of Joshua and Betsy's engagement. He asked Betsy if he could speak with her in private.

Powell and Betsy sat beneath a tree. He eyed her engagement ring and confessed that he was envious of Joshua's good fortune in winning her hand. Betsy grew uncomfortable at the attention, not to mention the confession. The only thing she could think to say was to promise Powell an invitation to the wedding.

Richard Powell remained a short time longer, talking to the picnickers and, perhaps, even soliciting the vote of the men in the upcoming election. Then he mounted his black horse and rode off.

After eating, the young couples each went their separate ways along the riverbank. Joshua and Betsy sat on a moss-covered ledge of rock overlooking a bubbling spring. Red River was full from spring rains and a bit muddy. Joshua had thrown in his fishing line, not really caring if he caught a fish or not. He propped the pole against a fallen log and anchored the end with a heavy rock. Then he turned his attention to Betsy.

Instantly, something like a huge fish grabbed the line, jerked the pole loose, and carried it upstream, where it made a U-turn and returned. Then a familiar voice rang out among the trees. "Please, Betsy Bell, do not marry Joshua Gardner." The plea was repeated a total of three times, then the voice gradually died away.

The old fear of what the witch might do to her or Joshua returned to Betsy. Some of the other couples had heard the witch's entreaties and had seen the horrified look on Betsy's face. All the joy went out of the party, and the group started for home.

Betsy was silent for a long time. Then she turned to Joshua and told him that their engagement must be broken. Joshua tried to plead his case to Betsy. He was not afraid of the witch—let her do her worst. He would protect Betsy.

But Betsy knew better. Not even Frank Miles, with all his strength, could have made a difference. Past history had proven that. Strength and determination meant little when dealing with the spirit. And Joshua could offer her even less protection than Frank. She was afraid that if she did marry Joshua the witch would make the rest of their lives miserable, as she had promised.

Betsy held out her hand and asked Joshua to take the ring from her finger. Tears clouded her eyes. It was the saddest day of her life.

After Joshua and Betsy parted company, Richard Powell began courting her in earnest. She succumbed to his advances, probably hesitantly at first because, being his former pupil, she still looked upon Powell as an authority figure. When the couple finally married in 1824, Powell treated Betsy well. The witch apparently had no objection to this match, because she never said anything either for it or against it.

Legend says that Powell had actually been married before—that he had married Esther Hays Scott in 1815. According to the story, she was about 18 years older than her young husband. When she died in 1821, that left Powell free to marry Betsy. Neither Charles Bailey Bell nor Harriet Parks Miller mentions this aspect of Richard Powell's life, however.

Powell did finally attain political office, serving as sheriff and as a Tennessee state senator. In 1837 he suffered a massive stroke. Several reversals of fortune later, the Powell family was nearly destitute. Not even the state of Tennessee—although it tried to help—could provide relief for Powell and his family. He died in 1848. In spite of their problems, Betsy said later that her marriage was a happy one.

In 1875, Betsy moved to Panola County, Mississippi,

where she took up residence at the home of a daughter. She died there in 1890, a very old woman. She never heard from the witch again.

Joshua Gardner became a successful farmer. When he lost Betsy, he moved to Henry County and then to Weakly County, where he established himself near the small town of Gardner Station (named after his brother). He married twice and died in 1887.

One day in early summer of 1821, as the Bell family was sitting around the fireplace after supper, something like a cannonball rolled down the chimney and out into the room. Then it burst like a smoke bomb.

"I am going," the voice of the witch cried out. "I am going and will be gone seven years. Good-bye to all!"

So the witch had finally departed—at least temporarily. She promised to return in seven years. There was no doubt in the mind of some family members that the witch *would* return. Drewry, for example, lived the rest of his life like a haunted man. He absolutely believed the witch would be back, although not necessarily in just seven years. In fact, he doubted seriously if she had departed at all. He listened for her voice every day until the day he died.

Drewry was greatly affected by the witch. The entity had abused him nearly as much as she had abused Betsy, but his afflictions were not as well known. Betsy—the sweet innocent young girl—had garnered far more sympathy and notoriety than her brother. Drewry had faded into the background, and no one really knew how much the haunting had affected him.

For his whole life Drewry remained a bachelor. The witch's objection to the marriage of Joshua and Betsy weighed heavily on his mind. He was afraid that if he, too, became engaged to be married the witch would try to interfere with that.

Lucy Bell, too, expected to hear the spirit's familiar voice at any time. She remained in the old home place, although most of her children scattered after the death of their father. By the time the witch returned in 1828, only Richard Williams and Joel Egbert lived with their mother.

When John Bell died, Lucy was given a widow's pension by the Robertson County court. This included a Negro named Dean (worth $500). She was also allowed 1200 pounds of bacon, 50 barrels of corn, 20 bushels of wheat, 75 pounds of lard, 50 pounds of sugar, ten pounds of coffee, and two stacks of fodder. She also received 106⅔ acres of her husband's land.

John Jr., the heir apparent, built a house near the home place and farmed his father's land. One evening in March 1828, he was sitting by his fire reading when, without so much as a by-your-leave, the familiar voice of the witch rang out, "John, I am in hopes you will not be as angry at me on this visit as you were on my last. I shall do nothing to cause you offense. I have been in the West Indies for seven years and...."

John Jr.'s attitude toward the witch had not mellowed one fig. "Your proper place is in hell," he declared as if he were picking up the conversation from where he and the witch left off seven years before. "The next visit you make you should go there and stay!"

The witch replied by telling John Jr., again, that she was an outcast. Then she went into a long, involved monologue about living people on the earth who were much worse than she was.

John Jr. offered no sympathy. "I would give my life freely if I could tangibly grasp your form in my arms and crush you slowly, giving you the pain you caused my father, and then throw you straight into the fires of hell!"

From this rather unfruitful beginning, the witch began her return visit—not to the Bell farm as before, but to the newly-built home of John Jr. Lucy Bell made contact with the witch only once on her return visit. The witch seemed nearly to have forgotten her.

No. This time the witch had a different agenda. She avoided any other contact in the neighborhood and kept her visit secret. Outside of the family, only Frank Miles knew of the witch's return.

The next night, the witch returned to Bell's home and found him rereading the plans for the Battle of New Orleans which he, of course, had participated in while serving under Andrew Jackson.

"There will be another battle at New Orleans," the witch said. "The city will be captured by a Tennessean. He is an officer in the U.S. Navy now, but he will be on the other side. This fight at New Orleans will determine you to go into the army against the North, but you will not realize your decision. You will depart from this world just after that battle at the city in which you've felt so interested."

Captain David G. Farragut captured New Orleans on April 25, 1862. On May 1, the North took control of New Orleans and southern Louisiana. They held the city for the rest of the war, thereby effectively blocking the mouth of the Mississippi River. Farragut was born near Knoxville in 1801. By 1828, when the spirit returned, he was a junior officer in the U.S. Navy. John Bell, Jr., although elderly when the Civil War began, determined that he would enlist in the Confederate Army. But before he could do so, he died of pneumonia on *May 8, 1862!*

"The United States will have wars, no doubt in your lifetime," the witch continued. "But with the exception of the one which will result in freedom for the Negroes, these will not be serious. That is, until a great war which will likely involve nearly the whole world.

"The United States, at that time, will have become one of the world's greatest nations. Therefore it will be drawn into this terrible struggle.

"Millions of men will be killed, countries left in financial straits, and years of suffering invade every nation. Many people, as usual when wars occur, will for a time profit and be accustomed to a life of gain and luxury. They will forget what the after results of such a great conflict would be.

"Your country will suffer morally, financially, spiritually, and thousands will suffer the want and necessities of life."

And then, after predicting World War I, the spirit turned around and predicted World War II: "There will be threats and signs of another great upheaval which, if it comes, will be far more devastating and fearful in character than the one the world thought too terrible for the mind to grasp." (Keep in mind that World War I was called "the war to end all wars.")

The spirit also predicted the end of the world. It told John Jr. that the temperature was the greatest factor in deciding whether a planet is inhabitable. According to the spirit, the heat on the surface of the planet would increase so rapidly in such a short time that humans could not bear it. Then the planet would be completely destroyed by a mighty explosion.

The spirit did not give an exact date of the end but indicated it would occur sometime in the twentieth century.

After having spent several months with John Jr., the spirit suddenly announced it was leaving the next night. It asked that Frank Miles also be present for the farewell, that it had something of the utmost importance to say.

The next night, promptly at 8:00 p.m., the spirit arrived and said, "To you two, who are inseparable friends, I say that whether the world ever hears of what I have told John or not, as bad as you both think I have been, I hope it will be recognized that what I have said to John is for the best. The world will so live.

"I shall be there. You two will know what I am doing. The world may not recognize spirits, whether good or demon. Both will be here. It will have many of each.

"Again, John, your descendants will not be worried by me,

but I promise you now if it is for their good, and I am allowed, for once I will be helpful to them and their country. I am bidding you and Frank a last farewell. I will be here again in another seven years, to which one hundred years will be added."

And then there was silence. Was the witch, at last, really gone? There are some who believe the witch never left in the first place.

CHAPTER SEVEN

Adams, Tennessee, lies about ten miles northwest of Springfield on Highway 41. In John Bell's time, this tiny town, named after merchant Reuben Adams, was called Adams Station. Today, only a few stores and gas stations remain open for business.

About a block from the blinking caution light are the remnants of the central business district. The area is about a block long and lined with the abandoned wooden storefronts that look like a set for a western movie. If you look carefully at the hand-painted sign on the front of one of the buildings, you can just barely make out the words "dry goods."

At one time, Adams was an important stop on the Louisville and Nashville Railroad. And Highway 41 was a major artery between Nashville and Hopkinsville, Kentucky. But when the interstate was built some years ago, I-24 cut Adams off from the rest of the world. Springfield survived because it was the county seat of Robertson County. Clarksville, located just west of I-24, is a large town because of its cozy proximity to Fort Campbell. But the nearby small towns of Sadlersville, Port Royal, and Cedar Hill are all but forgotten.

Yet, for the traveler willing to take a back road, Adams provides delightful surprises—especially in light of its association with the infamous Bell Witch. Spending time in and around Adams, picking up bits and pieces of the Bell Witch story, treading the ground where the events were supposed to have taken place, and keeping in mind the possibility that the witch may still walk those hills tends to give a person a severe case of the creeps.

Yet, with all the ghostly ambiance surrounding Adams, surprisingly little has been done in town to capitalize on its best-known citizen—the witch. In fact, there are only three businesses that attempt to make hay on the most famous haunting in Tennessee—maybe in the entire country.

The first is Mystery City, located just off Highway 41 by Red River. Second is the Bell Witch Cave.

Then entering Adams from the south, the Bell Witch Village and Antique Mall lies to the right. Nina Seeley, a former Nashville musician, owns this business located in the old Bell School. And every Saturday night the creaky old building rings with country music when the Bell Witch Opry shifts into overdrive.

Nina has played with music greats like Carl Perkins and Eddy Arnold. Her first husband, Kenneth, owned a farm near Adams. A country music fan, he wanted to help young people who longed to play music but did not have the money to take lessons. Nina suggested the pair start an "opry" so people could perform. They met with officials of radio station WDBL, who agreed to broadcast the concerts.

Nina Seeley is one of the locals who believe the Bell Witch is still active. In fact, she believes the witch haunts the old schoolhouse where the Opry is located. At night she hears mysterious noises upstairs in the creaking old schoolhouse, but when she investigates, nothing is there.

Some other locals believe the witch is still active in Robertson County. In fact, many are able to point to specific instances that substantiate their case. They say the witch is especially hard on scoffers—those who believe the story to be a myth. Perhaps Seeley's open declaration that the Bell Witch is real is her method of self-preservation.

One old gentleman from Adams agreed that ill always befalls people who claim there is no such thing as the Bell Witch—malfunctioning automobiles, failed electronic gadgets, important items mysteriously disappearing, even accidents and fires.

The late Wayne M. Eden, Jr.'s stories are especially intimidating, particularly for a person who wants to approach the Bell Witch story impartially. Eden owned that part of the Bell farm on which the Bell Witch Cave is located. Although some people thought Eden was inflicted with an incurable flair for the theatrical (after all he *was* trying to attract visitors to the cave), his tales of cars suddenly turning over for no reason, an enigmatic red spot that terrorized his daughter one night in her bedroom, and an unseen force latching on to him like a vise could raise goose pimples on a suit of armor.

A logical person might easily dismiss Eden's tales as pure bosh. But after talking with the current owner of the cave about her experiences, one is not so sure. At any rate, mystery piles upon mystery until even the sanest person finds himself uncertain of what is reality and what is not.

The exact location of John Bell's grave is as uncertain as the exact cause of his death. The old Bell family homestead is gone, and the nearby family graveyard is overrun in weeds and brambles. Most of the old granite grave markers have been stolen by souvenir hunters, and even the graves, themselves, show evidence of being disturbed. Since most of the markers were not inscribed with the names of those who lay beneath them, no one knows for sure who is buried where beneath the tangle of wild undergrowth. According to local legend, only John Bell's marker was inscribed.

As far as is known, only John Bell, Lucy, and about 30 Negro slaves are buried in the old plot. After the haunting was over, the children scattered—apparently wanting to get as far away from the old homestead as possible. So the Bell children are buried elsewhere.

But the spirits of those interred on the farm are apparently restless. At night, strange lights are reported and filmy apparitions appear to float over the old cemetery. Some claim the ghost of old John Bell, himself, haunts the land that he once owned and farmed, and on which he suffered so much.

In the early 1950s, as the story goes, three young men from Nashville happened upon the Bell graveyard late one night. Of course they knew the story of the Bell Witch, and when they saw the initials "J. B." carved on one of the rocks, they unwisely decided to take Bell's marker home as a keepsake.

On the way back to Nashville they were involved in an auto accident, and the driver of the car was killed. Within a week after the mishap, the two other boys also met with accidents.

The wrecked car was towed to the home of the parents of one of the boys. His sister was inspecting the car when she opened the trunk and noticed the granite marker still inside. She immediately knew what it was. Her blood ran cold. She realized the reason for the terrible tragedies that had befallen her brother and his friends.

She hastily put the heavy marker into her car and drove lickety-split back to Adams. But she had no idea where the Bell family graveyard was. So she stopped the car at a likely spot on a side road which she hoped, at least, was in the general vicinity of the family cemetery.

She removed the marker from her car and placed it on the ground beside the road. Then she hurriedly drove back to Nashville. If this story is true, then John Bell's original tombstone is covered with tangles of brush and is still sitting beside some half-forgotten country lane near Adams.

Carney Bell, a direct descendant, also has a tale to tell about ancestral cemeteries, and it was published in 1986 in a local newspaper:

This happened in 1975 or 1976. I was out rabbit hunting with four of my boys on the old Head farm about eight miles from the old family farm at Adams. One of my boys spotted a rabbit and took a shot at it. The rabbit rolled over as if it had been hit, then revived and ran off. We chased it into a honeysuckle thicket and lost it.

I put my hand down on what I thought was an old honeysuckle covered stump to get my feet untangled and when I did, I discovered it wasn't wood, but stone.

We took a closer look and found we were in an old, overgrown cemetery in the middle of the field and I had put my hand down on one of the old headstones.

The carving on it was almost gone. We rubbed a clod of dirt over the carving and saw that the name on the stone was Joel Egbert Bell—my great, great grandfather. I had been looking for that particular family grave for close to 20 years.

Strange about that incident. The witch had appeared as a rabbit before. Could it be possible that the witch, in the guise of a long-eared rodent, led Bell to that spot?

There is, however, one monument still standing in the original family cemetery as a silent sentinel to a man whose family was harassed and tortured beyond human endurance by an insidious creature from hell. This monument is inscribed:

Bell, John
1750-1820
Original tombstone disappeared about 1951.
This marker placed 1957.
His wife Lucy Williams Bell

Standing just east of the little town of Adams, on Tennessee Highway 41, is the Bellwood Cemetery. It was designed and built in the 1950s by Leslie Covington, a Bell descendant. Covington, a wealthy building contractor from Boston, paid for the project himself and set up a trust fund to insure the cemetery's eternal preservation. Its centerpiece is a large monument on which is inscribed a brief genealogical record of the Bell family:

John Bell 1750-1820 and his wife Lucy Williams
Pioneer Settlers from Halifax & Edgecombe Co., N.C.
Their children were
Jesse, John Jr., Drewry, Benjamin, Esther, Zadock, Elizabeth
Richard Williams and Joel Egbert

On another face of the monument is written:

John Bell, Jr. 1793-1862 and his wife Elizabeth Gunn
Their children were
Sarah Williams, Joel Thomas, Zadock, Martha Miles,
Mary Allen and John

On a third face is inscribed:

Joel Thomas Bell 1831-1910
and his wife Laura Virginia Henry
Their children were John Thomas, Flora Adeline, Sarah Elizabeth,
Boyd Minerva, Charles Bailey and Mary Allen

Although Charles Bailey Bell is buried at Bellwood Cemetery, along with his father, Dr. Joel Thomas (son of John Jr.), the main characters in this story are interred elsewhere— some in forgotten graves. But the trials and tribulations each experienced at the hands of the witch are not forgotten. In fact, if anything, more stories are being added every day.

CHAPTER EIGHT

Folklore, unlike dyed-in-the-wool history, does not merely consist of a set of dates, places, and events. Handed down orally from generation to generation, folklore is stories about people.

When John Jr. spent three days reciting the events of the haunting to his son, Joel, he was passing along folklore in its purest sense. Joel, of course, wrote down his father's reminiscences. Then he passed them along to his son, Charles Bailey. Later, Charles Bailey Bell used his father's notes to write his own book.

The oral tradition of tale telling is alive and well in Adams. I suspect that a full 50 percent of the current population can relate an account of a mysterious incident that happened either to them, a member of their family, or a close friend. Here is one of these tales:

One night C. G. was sitting in his living room, reading at his home outside Adams. His fireplace was burning brightly to ward off a chill in the air. The scene was a model of domestic tranquility. It was a dark and stormy night—wouldn't you just know it—and lightning flashes were so bright that it was almost like daytime.

Suddenly C. G. heard a wailing sound outside his door. At first he thought it might be his dog begging to get in. The German shepherd was scared to death of thunderstorms. But when he glanced around the living room, the dog was curled up by the fireplace. The animal, which also heard the wailing sound, got a funny look on his face, raised his head, and pricked up his ears.

C. G. opened the front door and peeked outside. Rain was falling so heavily that he could barely see the lights coming from the house across the road. A bright flash of lightning lit up the sky, enabling him to see nearby details. But there was no dog in sight.

C. G. closed the door, went back to the living room, and tried to return to his reading. He noticed his dog was shaking all over—something was frightening the animal.

Then C. G. got the uneasy feeling that he was not alone.

Just to be on the safe side, he reached for his shotgun and loaded the weapon with number nine buckshot. Then he went from room to room to flush out any intruder. He found nothing.

When he returned to the living room, C. G. found his dog, tail between his legs, back arched, cowering in a corner. The animal's eyes were showing white, and he was staring intently at something across the room.

In the opposite corner, beside the stone fireplace, a glowing ball of blue-white light hovered about four feet off the floor. A low hissing sound came from the ball, like red-hot coals sizzling.

Petrified that it might catch his house on fire, but afraid to approach it, C. G. watched the ball as it slowly rose up to about six feet. Then the light drifted toward the fireplace, pausing momentarily at the hearth. Then, in a sound like a cannon shot, the fireball flew up the chimney.

The dog bolted like he had been scalded and ran into the

bedroom, crawling underneath the bed. He refused to come out for the rest of the night.

"I've heard stories that the witch sometimes appears as a ball of fire," C. G. said. "Something or other was in that living room that night and scared me and my dog half to death. I'll lay you two-to-one odds it was the witch."

Indeed, strange balls of light *have been seen* at various intervals in and around Adams. One time, in the early part of the twentieth century, when parts of the Bell house were still standing, a group of young boys decided they would visit the old log cabin late one night.

They arrived shortly before midnight and walked inside the tumble-down building. Finding nothing out of the ordinary, they walked outside and looked across the little field. On the other side lay the Bell family graveyard.

The moon was out that night and the landscape was bathed in dim white light. Suddenly an iridescent ball of blue light rose from the old graveyard and began drifting across the field towards them. The boys froze in their tracks.

The ball stopped about 20 feet from where they were standing. A woman's voice seemed to come from it.

"Get ye away," the voice said sternly. "Ye have no business here."

Needless to say, the boys tarried no longer, picked up their feet, and moved smartly all the way back to Adams.

Then the tale is told of a family motoring along a back country road that skirted the Bell farm. Again it was dark, but this time cloudy.

Nothing seemed out of the ordinary as the father, mother, and their two children chatted happily about their just completed visit to the man's parents. Apparently the children's grandmother had baked a large batch of sugar cookies. Each child now held one in his pudgy hand, munching happily away. A half dozen more cookies were stashed in brown paper bags held in the other hand.

The man saw a set of headlights on the road ahead. It was a narrow road, as most secondary roads around Adams are. The headlights seemed to be coming straight down the middle of the road, and when they failed to move to the side or even slow down to let him pass, the man began to panic.

On both sides of the road were fields—no berm. The man was about to run off the road to avoid the oncoming auto. But the car was coming too fast. He estimated its speed at over 100 miles per hour.

"This is impossible," he thought only a split second before the two vehicles would strike. "There's a madman at the wheel."

The car was upon him. The man turned his wheel to the right. Too late. The pair of headlights racing toward him split just before they reached his car. One light passed on one side; the second light passed on the other. No sound of crunching metal. No collision.

The family car skidded to a halt, making a 180 degree turn in the middle of the road. The shaken driver peered out the windshield. He saw the two lights receding in the distance. His eyes widened in surprise. There was no car, where a car should have been, between them.

Sometimes braver souls will try to chase lights that sometimes appear near the old Bell farm. But their source, whatever it is, coyly avoids contact. Some folks have chased the lights, only to have them vanish, then reappear even farther away.

Most of these mysterious happenings are naturally blamed on the witch. She's a convenient scapegoat. And this kind of situation encourages pranksters. In 1961 an article appeared in the *Chicago Tribune* under the headline, "Bell Witch of Tennessee Reported Cavorting Again." In the piece, Robert M. Seals wrote:

The wild-eyed tales were making the rounds again not

long ago in the western suburbs when ghostly forms were seen—or were reported to have been seen—floating through the moonlit trees. There were other reports of weird cries in the night and unexplained rapping on the windows.

Practically all these recent recurrences, however, had been traced to pranks, because the last time the witch is known to have pestered the original Bell family was back in 1850 [?]. Because the legend of the Bell Witch is so well known the periodic outcrop of rumors would make it seem that every once in a while some prankster says to a friend, "Well, I guess it's time we brought the Bell Witch back."

There is no doubt in my mind that some of the Bell Witch stories are, indeed, the work of pranksters. The supernatural piques human interest like no other subject can.

People not only fear the supernatural, they are fascinated by it. Perhaps that is why tales of terror draw so many people into movie theaters. Perhaps that is why the shelf area of horror movies in tape rental stores is, in most establishments, larger than the area reserved for children's films. Perhaps that is why one of the best-selling authors of all time is Stephen King, and why Peter Straub and Anne Rice are such popular storytellers. Perhaps that is why one of the most popular tales at the annual National Storytelling Festival in Jonesborough, Tennessee, is the ghost story.

Whether or not they believe in ghosts or witches or demons, Americans are nevertheless fascinated with the possibility of their existence. There is a source of wonder in the supernatural—a totally unexplored territory in a world where nearly every corner has already been explored. This is especially true in the South.

Hans Holzer wrote in *The Phantoms of Dixie*:

The slower, more tradition-bound atmosphere of the Southern states tends to encourage a preoccupation with the occult.... The Southern states are less polyglot and in the main populated by people of Anglo-Saxon extraction. Now it is a fact that the Scottish, English, and Irish people have a greater leaning toward the psychic than have, let us say, the French and German nationals. Why this is so is difficult to determine unless, indeed, the Celtic heritage still pulsates in so many of these people. From their ancestral home in the British Isles many of these Southerners have derived a respect for the occult which makes them more receptive to reports dealing with occurrences of seemingly logical events. The atmosphere for ghosts, hauntings, psychic dreams and such is far more open in the South than in the urban North.

Dr. Sharon Turnbull, an educational psychologist, formerly with East Tennessee State University, said, "People need to have an explanation for events that are out of the ordinary. The explanation they choose might have to do with the supernatural. Others might choose an explanation to do with science, random events, fate, or whatever. But they need to have an explanation that they can believe—one that explains what happened, one that gives them some sort of cognitive control over it."

When classifying folktales, folklorists use a device called a "motif" or plot element. Some motifs are common to ghost stories—mysterious knockings on the walls, unseen footsteps, cold chills, ghosts hunting for lost gold, haunted houses, even ghosts hunting for missing parts of their anatomy, etc. Some motifs are not as common but are occasionally found in ghost lore—ghosts haunting skyscrapers for example.

A rarity in ghost lore is the "intelligent" ghost—one who thinks independently. The Bell Witch certainly fits this category. Above all, Kate was certainly articulate, thought for herself, and even exercised good common sense on occasion. In some ways the witch fits perfectly into the classic haunting mold with her banging and clangings. In other ways she breaks the mold to smithereens.

There is a certain amount of comfort in having your house haunted by a ghost that follows the rules of haunting—so-called ghost logic. Apparitions floating down hallways, cold spots, knockings on the walls, and footsteps tramping over-head are the things that traditional ghosts are supposed to do. And ghosts certainly do not beat people up, much less kill them. For the most part, traditional ghosts mind their own business, do their own thing, and appear only occasionally.

But it doesn't appear that the Bell Witch was a traditional ghost. In none of the available literature is she even referred to as a ghost. Mostly she's called a "spirit" or the "witch." As such, she adds a new—and frightening—dimension to the term "paranormal activity."

She is dangerous!

The most unsettling aspect about the witch is that she still seems to be active, still powerful, and no one knows where she'll show up next. There is one place in Robertson County where she apparently centers her activities—the creepiest, most haunted place of all—the Bell Witch Cave.

CHAPTER NINE

Some people swear up and down that the Bell Witch lives in the Bell Witch Cave, located on a bluff overlooking Red River. Judging from the number of strange incidents that have occurred in and around the cave, that particular notion may, indeed, be fact.

However, little is mentioned about the cave in contemporary accounts of the Bell Witch infestation, except that her voice was often heard in the vicinity along Red River. In the days before refrigeration, the cave was probably used by the Bell family as cold storage. Its constant temperature of 56 degrees helped keep perishables fresh, and it was considerably larger than any root cellar. It was also explored by adventurous youths, such as Betsy's friend who got stuck in one of the narrow passages and was rescued by the witch.

Today, of course, the original Bell house is no more. So Kate would not be able to haunt that. Perhaps the cave is a viable alternative for a homeless spirit looking for a place to lurk. At least, judging from the stories floating around Robertson County, that, indeed, seems to be the case.

In October 1986, a reporter and staff photographer from

It is said the entrance to the Bell Witch Cave is extremely difficult to photograph because it is alleged to be the home of the witch. This photo taken by a commercial photographer seems to be the best available print of the entrance. After a heavy rain, water gushes out of the entrance and flows through the riverbed at left. (Photo courtesy of Walter and Chris Kirby)

The Tennessean newspaper decided to spend the night in the Bell Witch Cave to see if the stories about it were true. Their report was published in the October 27 issue, just in time for Halloween.

Reporter David Jarrard admitted being primed for the visit. Two brothers (not named by Jarrard, but probably Paul and James Eden), who lived on the farm where the cave was located, regaled the visiting journalists and their cohorts with a legion of stories about the witch and the cave.

"We had been given permission to spend the night," Jarrard wrote, "but the brothers said they didn't think we should. They would never spend the night in the cave, they said."

Undaunted, the intrepid reporter and photographer pressed on. They passed by the heavy iron gate that guarded the entrance and entered the cave. The photographer, an experienced spelunker, swept the beam of his flashlight over the surroundings. Then he turned to Jarrard.

"You know," he said, "it's not the witches in this cave that I'm afraid of. Do you know what a brown recluse spider looks like?"

His flashlight beam fell on a gaggle of *Loxosceles reclusi* scrambling over a nearby rock. Suddenly a very unspider-like sound emerged from the bowels of the cave. Jarrard described it as "a raspy, deep sound like an unwavering groan, or a big electric buzzer with a weak battery." Then there came a series of heavy "thumps."

"I have never heard a noise like that in a cave before," the photographer said nervously. "*That* is not a cave noise."

There was another noise, a growling that seemed to come from just around the corner. At that point, a night in the cave became unattractive, the presence of the spiders providing a convenient excuse. But, after all, the Fourth Estate had journeyed all this way to get a Halloween story. So it was decided to stay just a little longer to see what else might happen.

For 15 minutes they sat quietly in the first room and listened for any other unusual sound. At first there was only the monotonous drip-drip of water. Then they heard a rumbling overhead that sounded like thunder, or maybe a jet plane passing. A walk to the iron gate might confirm suspicions.

As they neared the mouth of the cave, they could hear the jet more plainly, and began to relax. At least *one of the noises* they had heard had a logical explanation! Unfortunately, their complacency ill-prepared them for the next and final shock.

From far back in the cave there came a scream. "It was a short, powerful burst of sound that reverberated from the back of the cave and hit us like a slap," Jarrard wrote. "It was not a metallic screech or the howl of wind. It was a vocal, loud, high-pitched scream.

"We looked at each other, got through the gate and quickly left the cave behind us."

The cave's owner at the time of the visit was the late Wayne M. Eden, Jr., known far and wide as "Bims." He held that the Bell Witch legend was true and said that strange occurrences were still happening around the old Bell farm, especially in the vicinity of the cave.

The Bell Witch Cave is small, as most commercial caves go. Because of narrow passageways, visitors can travel only about 500 feet from its entrance. Its exploitability is based on the Bell Witch stories and the odd things that occur inside. Bims tried to improve the cave's interior by adding electric lights, but he did little else. His main occupation was farming, growing tobacco and corn.

Still, undeveloped as it was, the Bell Witch Cave attracted thousands of visitors who wanted to be shown through. Somehow they located the cave—there were no signs to point the way. Bims, apparently, was happy to show them around and tell stories—some based on his own experience.

In 1980 Bims had put the cave up for sale. He said that he wanted to spend more time farming and less time answering questions about the Bell Witch. His asking price: $999,500.

Bims had owned the farm about 17 years but had lived on various parts of the old Bell place for 40 years. He and his wife, Myrtle, had dwelt in various farmhouses on the place and could recount an extensive list of strange incidents that had occurred in them.

Every house that he had lived in on the old Bell farm came equipped with knocking noises, Bims explained in a 1981 newspaper interview. "Sometimes when you go to the door, there is someone there. Other times, there's not," he said.

Knockings were the least of Bims's experiences. One year about an inch of snow fell on Robertson County. Bims heard someone knocking at his front door. He looked through the window and saw a figure that he did not recognize walking away from the house. It walked behind a tree but did not emerge on the other side.

Bims grabbed his shotgun and went outside to investigate. He found no one, not even footprints in the fresh snow!

On another occasion, Bims was awakened from a sound sleep by his daughter, Mary, calling to him. When he went to her room he saw a red spot hovering about four feet off the floor. She confessed that the spot had been deviling her for quite some time but that she was afraid to tell anyone for fear that it might "get" her.

The spot has never been explained.

When Bims finally got tired of living in old, haunted farmhouses, he tore down one of the original Bell family dwellings and built a modern one-story brick home. A few years later, he died in the house.

Present owners of the Bell Witch Cave include a young

couple, Walter and Chris Kirby. Walter is a tobacco farmer. The Bell Witch story fascinates Chris because of her interest in history.

Chris said they had been looking for a farm for years. But she, being a city girl, was reluctant to move to the country. "You find me something I can do too," she told him, "then I'll move."

Finding the farm that included the historic Bell Witch Cave was a godsend for the couple. The land was purchased from the Eden estate, and the Kirbys moved in April 1993. By summer they had the cave open to the public. (Bims Eden never had sold the cave. Chris thinks it was priced too high.)

I asked Chris if she has heard any noises yet.

"We've heard them in the cave. We've heard them in the house. I feel like if there's any place that could be haunted (or should be haunted), it's this place here. First of all it's got a 180-year-old legend of being haunted. There's an Indian burial ground right above the mouth of the cave on the bluff. And the previous owner of the cave died in our bedroom."

Frightening, unexplained things occur in the Bell Witch Cave. Here's an example:

One day Chris was in the middle of a tour. She owned a golden retriever, who accompanied her on all her cave tours. Once inside, the dog would splash happily in the water that ran through the cave's mouth.

As soon as Chris opened the steel gate at the entrance of the cave, she began to hear weird noises. "It sounded like it was all around me—like someone with asthma breathing down a pipe. That real raspy breathing. I only heard it for a second."

Chris turned to the people who were with her. They were standing in a group, talking, and hadn't heard a thing.

The tour continued through the first room and finally made it through to the second. At the back of the cave, Chris was telling Bell Witch stories and pointing out some of the formations.

"Suddenly the dog just went nuts. Her hair stood up on her back, she showed her teeth and started growling. She acted vicious. I had never seen her act like that before. She was growling and barking. But there was nothing there."

The tour group asked what the dog was barking at.

"I don't know," Chris answered.

Finally Chris coaxed the dog to her side. Then the animal started whining, her tail tucked between her legs. Suddenly Chris's flashlight went out.

"I thought there must be a logical explanation," Chris said. "It could have been the bulb. But right after that a lady's video camera suddenly stopped working. And there we were in the dark. That was one time I was scared. I was ready to leave and so was everybody else."

I asked Chris if the dog ever acted like that in the cave again.

"Yeah," she answered. "Other times she'd go in there with me, as far as the first room, and she'd start whining. I'd call her and call her, but I couldn't get her to go any further. She'd run out of the cave."

The Bell Witch Cave can be reached by turning from Highway 41, just past the Bell School, onto Bell Chapel Road and by following the signs. After traveling three-tenths of a mile down a gravel road, making a sharp bend by a tobacco barn, you reach a one story brick house. A sign immediately in front says "Bell Cave Parking."

The cave is open from May 1 to October 31, 10 a.m. to 6 p.m., seven days a week.

To the right of the parking lot is a large sinkhole caused when a part of the cave collapsed. Chris said that when the air outside is very cold, vapor rises from fissures in the sinkhole because the air inside remains at a constant 56 degrees.

The cave is reached by walking across the Kirbys' backyard and down a gravel path, which descends down the face of the bluff toward the river. (The path was recently blocked when a gigantic ice storm brought down limbs and even whole trees.) The Kirbys improved the path because the original, built by Eden, was so narrow that one misstep could send the hiker hurtling down the cliff and into the river.

The Bell Witch Cave is actually located almost in the center of the bluff, about 30 feet above the swirling Red River. In the wintertime, or in exceedingly wet periods, water gushes from the mouth and spills over the edge of the bluff, creating a spectacular waterfall. For this reason, the cave is closed to visitors from November to May.

A quick inspection of the waterway between the cave entrance and the brink of the falls shows the flow occasionally reaches a depth of four feet or more.

The cave, itself, juts back from the face of the bluff at a sharp angle. No one really knows how extensive the Bell Cave really is. Visitors can be taken only to the first two rooms—a distance of about 500 feet.

About 30 feet from its mouth is a locked iron gate that is supposed to prevent unauthorized visitors from entering. But Chris told me that in their first six weeks of owning the cave, they experienced two break-ins.

The Bell Witch Cave is an irresistible magnet for young men who seek adventure, or who want to give their girlfriends a good scare. Canoeists on Red River pull their boats on shore just below the cave entrance, climb the bluff, and try to enter. Although the gate is constructed of heavy-duty steel bars, it doesn't offer total resistance to determined trespassers.

Chris worries that people will hurt themselves if allowed to run around the cave without supervision. Numerous nooks and crannies, some barely large enough for people to wiggle through, could be death traps.

The iron gate and the mouth of the cave are extremely difficult to photograph. This is, of course, attributed to the witch who is rumored to live inside. And sometimes strange images appear on photographic film.

"People take pictures inside and outside the cave all the time," Chris said. "And they would call me up later and tell me about the strange things that showed up in their pictures."

Visitors have sent her copies of the photos. And she has even taken some very odd pictures herself—like the time a devil-like "face" showed up in a photo taken of the sinkhole (see page xi).

And then there are the sounds...always the sounds....

One Halloween, a cave explorer was helping the Kirbys with an overflow crowd. That night he had a group of about 12 people in the first room. They heard a noise—the spelunker said everybody in his group heard it.

When the group finally emerged from the cave, the spelunker began telling of the experience. Suddenly Chris's brother-in-law asked, "Did it sound like a screen door?"

"Yes," the spelunker answered. "How did you know?"

"I heard it in there about a week ago when I was doing repair work on the lights," he answered.

I asked Chris whether the mysterious happenings in the cave made her nervous.

"Yeah, in some ways," she answered. "But I go in the cave all the time."

"By yourself?" I asked.

"No, I won't go in there by myself. I've never been in there by myself, and I won't go in there by myself. Furthermore, I don't mind being on the property, or in my house, in the daytime. But I won't be left here at night by myself! We hear weird noises...."

I asked Chris to elaborate.

One night the Kirbys were lying in bed talking. Suddenly

they heard a noise like someone moving a refrigerator across the basement floor. Both sat up in bed.

"What was that?" Chris said.

"Just listen," Walter answered.

They heard the noise again.

"It's coming from the basement," Chris whispered. "Let's go down and see what it is."

But Walter remained where he was. "Just listen," he suggested.

The sound had apparently stopped, because nothing else was heard. "It was probably nothing," Walter said.

"But we both heard it," Chris declared. "And it was awfully loud to be nothing!"

A few weeks after that incident, Chris was standing on a chair, changing a light bulb in the kitchen. A glass globe fitted over the light and was held fast by decorative screws.

When she attempted to replace one of the screws, it slipped out of her fingers and fell to the floor. Fortunately, Chris had sharp eyes and was able to track the screw as it bounced over toward a corner. She climbed down off the chair and went over to retrieve it, but the screw was gone.

"I thought that it might have bounced and rolled somehow," Chris said. "I bet I spent 30 minutes looking around that kitchen. I even got my dust mop and ran it under everything, looking for that screw, but I couldn't find it.

"So I went downstairs to the basement and found another screw that would work until I found a replacement.

"During the next three weeks, I cleaned the whole kitchen several times, mopped and swept, and even vacuumed. I had totally forgotten about the screw.

"One day we were working outside and I had to go to the kitchen to get some water. I walked in the side door and the screw was lying right in the middle of the floor. I had lost it in a corner, and there it was in the middle of the floor! The screw is black and the floor is kind of white, so it showed up real good.

"Have you ever been in a room," Chris continued, "and had your back turned toward a doorway, and all of a sudden you can feel someone looking at you or feel a presence? Well, there are times that I've been in the house and I've been busy doing something and I could suddenly feel someone watching me. I would turn around expecting to see my daughter, Candy. But there's nobody there. But you can feel the presence. It just kind of makes your skin crawl."

Chris said that her husband, Walter, doesn't like to go into the cave by himself either. In fact, he hesitates to even go near it!

"He avoids the cave as much as he can," she said. "He says that every time he goes in the cave he gets horrible headaches."

I suggested that Walter might be claustrophobic. Chris disagreed.

"He said as far as being inside, that doesn't bother him. But he said he always gets these horrible headaches. And he always gets hurt when he's down there. He hit his head real hard in there one time and got a big old knot. Another time he reached over to pick up something and messed up his back. He was out of work for a week.

"He works on a freight dock, so he packs freight all the time. He never has trouble with his back.

"He told me that every time he comes down to the cave he either gets hurt or gets a headache. So he doesn't like coming down here."

Chris even finds human bones on her farm these days. Shortly after moving to the farm, Chris's golden retriever began to bring the bones home.

At first the Kirbys thought they were animal bones. When they suddenly appeared in the yard or on the porch, Chris would toss them into the sinkhole.

Then one day the Kirbys were cleaning out an old smoke-house and discovered a large cache of skeletal remains stashed in a corner. Walter studied the bones carefully, then said, "These are human."

The Kirbys called the Robertson County Sheriff's Department. They arrived at the Kirby farm, took one look at the bones they had found, and transported them to the hospital in Springfield so the doctors there could examine them. The doctors verified they were human bones—and very old.

Then a Tennessee state archeologist visited the Kirby farm. He, too, declared the bones were human. They were Indian bones, he said, between 1,000 and 2,000 years old! One of the bones, a jaw complete with teeth, was from a man over 40 years old at the time of his death.

These bones were the remains of mound builders who had populated Robertson County long before the white man ever arrived—some of which who lived there at the time of Christ!

The archeologist told Chris that it is illegal in Tennessee to keep any human remains in private possession. He said a Native American association would take charge of the bones and reinter them complete with an appropriate ceremony.

AFTERWORD

People living in the 1990s like to think of themselves as "enlightened." Belief in ghosts, like being a slave to superstition, is seen by many as a product of the dark ages. Belief in ghosts, demons, witches, etc. is often considered the exclusive province of the lunatic fringe.

In folklore, unlike authenticated history, the story is more important than cold, hard facts. Since few of the Bell Witch happenings can be proved, we must rely almost solely on folklore to tell the story. At the same time, we must also rely on the honesty and integrity of the tellers of the various tales—living or dead.

Folklorists, especially we who specialize in ghost tales, are considered a little strange. Occasionally we are mistaken for ghost hunters, investigators of haunted houses, or shameless cavorters with familiar spirits. Armchair historians sometimes like to refer to folklorists as "semi-serious" collectors of tall tales.

Sober-minded people of the 1990s may declare openly they don't believe in ghosts. But isn't it strange how the tale of the Bell Witch of Tennessee refuses to die, and isn't it also strange how a notable number of scoffers refuse to emphatically declare that she doesn't exist? Dare we resurrect the old adage about "where there's smoke, there's fire"?

To me, first and foremost, the story is the thing. When I can, I squeeze a little history into the story. But too much history, like too much folklore, can be a drug. The reader, as well as the writer, can overdose.

My goal is to strike a balance—a happy medium if you will—so that one never outweighs the other. On one hand, we have a roaring good ghost story—on the other, an easily digestible historical sketch of early frontier life in Tennessee and Robertson County.

And we must not forget our sociology. People lived much differently in the days of John Bell. They had a different set of values, were more introspective, and—most important— had a different point of reference. There were few diversions to distract them—no television, radios, movies, Super Nintendo, or senior proms. Even newspapers were rare.

The Bible was the main reading matter on the frontier. A family's status in the community depended on how faithfully they attended church. Biblical lessons in morality formed the basis of frontier philosophy. Satan, the source of all evil, was believed to have an army of minions on earth to do his dirty work and to tempt the living. Presbyterian, Baptist, and Methodist beliefs of the time emphasized that anything not of God—and that included the Bell Witch—was of the devil.

Strangely enough, these same people, in spite of their prohibitions against it, were more attuned to the supernatural than we are today. There was widespread belief that ghosts haunted houses and demons bedeviled the living. A family plagued by some supernatural denizen was probably a family that had moved away from God and spirituality. Hence the haunting constituted a just reward for their sins—a good old Calvinist outlook.

I find it not surprising that John Bell's expulsion from Red River Baptist Church—no matter the stated reason—was probably due to the widespread belief among the faithful that their elder's life was in a terminal state of spiritual disorder. His alleged business misdealing with Kate Batts and her husband was only one example. But when his house was disrupted by an entity of supernatural origin, that put the lid on the buttermilk. God was personally dealing with the wayward Mr. Bell.

In those days, expulsion was a societal death sentence. It is greatly to the credit of preacher Sugg Fort that he remained supportive of John Bell during both the actions of the church and the activity of the witch. Fort was a rock! Even the witch liked and respected him. Unlike most of his flock, Fort was not a judgmental man.

In 1828 the witch departed the Bell farm for the last time. Most of the family had moved from the old home place by then, and only Lucy and two of her sons, Joel Egbert and Richard Williams, remained. Betsy had married Richard Powell, and Lucy was happy to see the marriage working out so well, in spite of the difference in their ages.

Lucy Bell died in 1837 and was buried beside her husband in the family graveyard. Long before this, however, visitors had stopped coming. There was nothing more to see or hear in the Bell house—only stories to be passed down from generation to generation.

After Lucy's death, the old house was deserted and never lived in again. For a time it was used to store grain, but it was eventually torn down.

Remaining members of the Bell family continued to keep their silence about the witch and wished no further publicity. When they did talk, which was mostly to their own children, they referred to the witch's visit as "our family trouble."

In 1849, many years after the haunting, the *Saturday*

Evening Post published an article about the Bell Witch phenomenon. The piece insinuated that the whole affair was engineered by Betsy Bell herself. Betsy, angered beyond reason, slapped a libel suit on the *Post*. Since the charges in the article were based on speculation, at best, and to avoid a large financial settlement, the publication retracted and the matter never went to court.

Fifty years later, M.V. Ingram published his *Authenticated History of the Bell Witch*, a fanciful tale based, for the most part, on the remembrances of Joel Egbert Bell, the youngest son of John Sr. Joel was about four years old when the haunting began and eight when the witch left. Ingram also used a diary written by Richard Williams Bell, who was not much older than his brother during the haunting.

According to Charles Bailey Bell, the rest of the family was outraged that Ingram published his book. They did not believe "the time had come for any publication about the witch. My father declined emphatically to disclose anything he knew, telling me at that time his father's [John Jr.'s] recollections, when published, were such as would give our most intelligent people an insight into the spirit world. He said that he thought Richard Williams's manuscript was true, but he was too young at the time to understand the spirit. Certainly the spirit could not disclose to him the wonderful things related to John Jr...."

On the other hand, Carney Bell, a direct descendant of the Bell family, told me that when Charles Bailey Bell published his own version of the story in 1934, the rest of the family was appalled. They refused to speak to him and thought he was a "real scoundrel."

Carney Bell said that the Bell family is now beginning to lighten up about the witch. Some of the Bells don't mind talking about the witch anymore because they are so far removed from the haunting. However, he says he has a sister who still will not discuss it. "She simply doesn't believe it," he said.

As for himself, Carney Bell takes the story with a grain of salt. "There is no doubt in my mind that the events my ancestors suffered were quite real to them," he said.

I think Carney Bell was speaking for all of us when he expressed this opinion. When the night is dark, when strange noises are heard, minds conjure up terrifying visions of unspeakable horrors. In that respect, we are no different from the Bells. The big difference, of course, is that most of our fears are fleeting. All indications point to the fact that the Bell Witch was very real!

The horror inflicted on this family, however, has lasted almost 200 years. They lived it, they believed it. But is the haunting really over? To those who have experienced the mysterious events that happen almost daily in and around the little town of Adams, it's still an open question.

To people like Chris Kirby, who continues to refuse to enter the Bell Witch Cave alone, the possibility the Bell Witch is still active is very much on her mind.

And Nina Seeley claims strange noises occur on the second floor of the old Bell School that houses her antique shop. When you talk to her about the possibility that it is the witch making the noises, you just can't miss the little-girl wonder that fills her face when she declares, "I just *know* it's the Bell Witch. I believe in her."

INDEX

witch what he thinks of her 41-42; accuses witch of really being an outcast demon 42; 47; relationship with witch 63, 64-65; reaction to haunting 65; decides to talk to son about witch 65; biography 65; reaction to Betsy's abuse 66; policy of non-interference 66; discovers unconscious body of father 74; discovers strange medicine in cabinet, tests it on cat 74-75; reaction to witch's return 81; 90; 91; 113

BELL, JOHN, Sr. (son of William): 1; biography 7-9; personal philosophy of life 13-14; thinks earthquakes cause noises 15; religious beliefs of 16; convicted of usury 16, 30; expelled from church 18; thinks disturbances caused by vandals 18; inflicted with physical ills 19; searches for lost Indian tooth 23; suffers bodily contortions 25; abuse given by witch 25-26; said to have murdered Kate Batts 30; on making loans to neighbors 30; visitors come to see witch 34; worries over Lucy's illness 40; greets Andrew Jackson 48; 52; 59; reaction to witch 62; physical afflictions 73; incident at pigsty 73-74; predicts own death 74; found unconscious by sons 74; strange medicine 74-75; death of 75; funeral of 76; location of grave 87-88; ghost of 88; boys steal his marker 88; grave marker of 89; 90; 111; 112

BELL, JOHN THOMAS (son of Joel Thomas): 90

BELL, LAURA VIRGINIA HENRY (wife of Joel Thomas): 90

BELL, LUCY (wife of John Sr.): 33; kind treatment by the witch 38-40; Betsy reports to her about seeing witch 50-51; 54; tries to get rid of witch 60-62; expects witch to return at any time 81; given widow's pension by Robertson County Court 81; 82; location of gravesite 88; grave marker of 89; 90; death of 112

BELL, MARTHA MILES (daughter of John Jr.): 90

BELL, MARY ALLEN (daughter of Joel Thomas): 90

BELL, MARY ALLEN (daughter of John Jr.): 90

BELL, RICHARD WILLIAMS (son of John Sr.): age when disturbances began 14; describes strange noises 14-15; on witch as busybody 21-22; on rabbit hunt 51; rescued from storm by witch 57-58; writes of visitors to Bell house 72; 81; 90; 112; 113

BELL, SARAH ELIZABETH (daughter of Joel Thomas): 90

BELL, SARAH WILLIAMS (daughter of John Jr.): 90

BELL SCHOOL (Adams): 86

BELL, WILLIAM (father of John Sr.): tells stories to son 8

BELL WITCH: place in Tennessee history vii; predicted return vii; overturned car attributed to vii-viii; stopped car attributed to viii-x; identifies self 3; 9; modern-day appearance in mirror to little girl 10-11; makes first noises 14-15; typical sounds 19; begins to talk 20; gives James Johnson nickname 20; as local busybody 20-22; on its own identity 22, 23; on buried treasure 23; determined to kill John Bell 25; abuses John Bell 25-26; follows Betsy to Thorn house 33; takes Betsy's friends on wild sleigh ride 34; taunts Frank Miles 35-37; abuses Drewry Bell 37; kind treatment of Lucy Bell 38-40; talks to John Jr. about punishment of Betsy, her unhappiness, and Lucy Bell 41; talks about the nature of fools 42; stops Andrew Jackson's horses and wagon 47-48; cuts "witch tamer" down to size 48-49; confronts Betsy in woods 50-51; participates in rabbit hunt 51; pays Joshua Gardner left-handed compliment 51-52; harasses Joshua and Frank Miles 52-54; pleads with Betsy not to marry Joshua 55, 78; rescues boy from cave 56, 98; could be kind to Betsy 56; a birthday surprise 56-57; effects rescue from violent storm 57-58; behavior of witch 58-59; as a disciplinarian of slaves 59-60; beats up the slave Harry 59; forces Harry to chop wood 59-60; dislike of Negroes 60; foils plot to get rid of her 60-62; attacks Anky 61-62; reacts to reactions 62-63; sassed by John Jr. 63; reaction to John Jr. 64; behavioral traits 66-67; tells John Jr. why she is against marriage of Betsy and Joshua 67; on divinity of Jesus Christ 68; why she considers Napoleon a Christian 68-69; on power struggle in Europe 69; on President James Monroe and the Monroe Doctrine 70-71; taunts John Sr. at pigsty 73; claims she poisoned John Sr. 75; taunts John Sr. on deathbed 75; attends John Sr.'s funeral 76; leaves Bell house for first time 80; returns in 1828 81; predicts War Between The States 82; predicts John Jr.'s death 82; predicts WWI 83; predicts WWII 83; predicts end of the world 83; promises to return again in 107 years 84; analysis 96-97

H

HALIFAX COUNTY (N. C.): 8

HALL, CORBAN (the elder): settles Robertson Co. 7

HALL, CORBAN (the younger): finds Indian jawbone 23;

"HARRY" (Bell slave): 59-60

HENDERSON, RICHARD: 4

HENRY CO. (Tenn.): 80

HOLSTON RIVER (Tenn.): 6

HOLZER, HANS (writer): on Southern ghost tradition 95-96

HOPKINSVILLE (Ky.): 85

HOPSON, DR. GEORGE: tries to treat John Bell 26; tries to save John Bell 74-75

HORSESHOE BEND (Ga.): 47

HOUSE OF REPRESENTATIVES, U.S.: 46

I

INDIAN WARS: outbreak and peace conference of 1777 4; harassment of whites 6; raid on Nashboro 6

INGRAM, M. V.: writes *Authenticated History of the Bell Witch*, much to disgust of Bell family 113

INTERSTATE 24: effect of cutting off small towns 85-86

J

JACKSON, ANDREW (father of Andrew): dies 43

JACKSON, ANDREW: 12; biography 43-47; attitude toward witch 43; known for volatile temper 46; fights duel with Charles Dickinson 46; investigates Bell Witch 47-50; 65

JACKSON, ELIZABETH HUTCHINSON (mother of Andrew): wants son to be a minister 43

JACKSON RACHEL DONELSON (wife of Andrew): is insulted by Charles Dickinson 46

JACKSON, ROBERT (brother of Andrew): enters military prison and dies of smallpox 44

JESUS CHRIST: witch discusses divinity of 68-69

JOHNSON, ISAAC: escapes from Indians, 6

JOHNSON, JAMES: settles Robertson Co. 7; investigates haunting 19-20; hunts treasure 23; witch's high regard for 59

JOHNSON, JOHN: settles Robertson Co. 7; joins John Bell deathwatch 74

JONESBOROUGH (Tenn.): Andrew Jackson practices law there 44; 95

K

KILGORE, THOMAS: 1; settles Robertson

County, Tenn., 5-6

KILGORE'S STATION (Tenn.): 5; abandoned to Indians and reclaimed 7

KING, STEPHEN (writer): 90

KIRBY, CHRIS (co-owner of Bell Cave): photographs sinkhole xiv, 106; buys Bell Witch Cave 103; her dog goes crazy inside cave 103-104; hears heavy object moving across basement floor 106; loses, then finds mysterious screw 107-108; feels presence in the house 108; finds old bones 108-109; 114

KIRBY, WALTER (husband of Chris): avoids cave 108

KNOXVILLE (Tenn.): 82

L

LAFFITE, JEAN: 47

LAND: George III sets boundaries 3-4

LEGREE, SIMON: 60

LITTLE TENNESSEE RIVER (in N. C.): Indian settlement along 4

LOUISIANA, State of: 82

LOUISVILLE AND NASHVILLE RAILROAD: 85

M

MARTIN, SAMUEL: captured by Indians 6

McCAY, SPRUCE: Andrew Jackson studies law with 44

MENEES, ISAAC: settles in Robertson Co. 7

MILES, FRANK: physical description 35; encounters with witch 35-37; is bested in test of strength 52-54; 66; curses witch 75; 83

MILLER, HARRIET PARKS (author): 29; 79

MISSISSIPPI RIVER: 11; perils of travel on 12-13; effect of 1811 earthquake on 15; 82

MISSISSIPPIAN INDIANS: nature of mounds 3; old bones found by Chris Kirby 109

MONROE DOCTRINE: witch predicts 70-71

MONROE, JAMES: witch discusses 70-71

MONTGOMERY CO. (Tenn.): founded 7

MONTGOMERY'S POINT (on Mississippi): 12-13

MOUND BUILDERS (see Mississippian Indians)

MYSTERY CITY (Adams): 86

N

NAPOLEON (BONAPARTE): witch explains why she thinks he is a Christian 68-69

NASHBORO (see Nashville)

NASHVILLE (Tenn.): changes name 5; Indian raid on 6, 7; Andrew Jackson takes over as Attorney General 44; 50; 85

NATIONAL STORYTELLING FESTIVAL: 90

NAVY, U. S.: 82
NEW MADRID FAULT: 15
NEW MADRID (Ill.): 12
NEW ORLEANS (La.): 12-13; first battle of 12, 47, 65; Blount orders Jackson to reinforce at 46; Blount orders Jackson to go a second time 47; second battle of 82
NOLICHUCKY RIVER (Tenn.): 6

O
OHIO RIVER: 11, 12

P
PANOLA CO. (Miss): Betsy Bell moves to 80
PERKINS, CARL (singer): 86
PHOTOGRAPHS: Bell Witch cave entrance x-xi; sinkhole xiv
PHOTOGRAPHY, SPIRIT: description and history of xi-xiii
PIERSON, ALISON (accused Scottish witch): burned 8
PIRATES (on the Mississippi): 12-13
PLUM POINT (on Mississippi River): 12
POLTERGEIST ACTIVITY: in Bell house 18
PORT ROYAL (Tenn.): as major shipping point 2; 6; as port 12; 26; 74; 85
PORTER, ALEXANDER: flatboats to New Orleans 12-13
PORTER, BENNETT: hunts treasure 23
PORTER, REBECCA: rescued from storm by witch 57-58
POWELL, RICHARD: educates Betsy Bell and Joshua Gardner 52; falls in love with Betsy 25, 54; drops in on picnic and makes feeling known to Betsy 76-78; becomes earnest suitor of Betsy, she marries him 79; has been married before 79; later life 79; 112
PRESBYTERIANISM: on frontier 16, 111

R
RED RIVER BAPTIST CHURCH: expels John Bell 18; 20; holds revival 28-30; 112
RED RIVER (Tenn.): as it is today 2; as useful waterway 2-3, 11-12; middle fork 5; 23; storm along 57-58; 76; 86
REELFOOT LAKE (on the Mississippi): created 15
REID, YOLANDA (Robertson Co. Historian): acquaintance with Willett and Gardner x; xiv
REVIVAL, THE GREAT: philosophy of 16-18
REVIVALS: at Red River Baptist Church 28-30
REVOLUTIONARY WAR: Andrew Jackson's service in 44
RIPPY, AGNES: incident with car viii, xiv

ROANE, ARCHIBALD: appoints Andrew Jackson a major general 46
ROBERTSON COUNTY CIRCUIT COURT: John Bell convicted of usury 18, 30
ROBERTSON COUNTY SHERIFF'S DEPARTMENT: called to investigate old bones 109
ROBERTSON COUNTY (Tenn.): history of 1; appearance today 1-3; caves beneath 2; home of Mississippian Indians 3; formed and settlement of 7; farm products 12; 57; 76; awards Lucy Bell a widow's pension 81; roads in 85; belief in witch 86; 97; 98; 111
ROBERTSON, JAMES: 4; helps settle French Lick 4-5

S
SADLERSVILLE (Tenn.): 85
SALISBURY (N. C.): Andrew Jackson studies law there 44
SATAN: 111
SATURDAY EVENING POST (nineteenth century magazine): insinuates that Betsy Bell is behind witch 113
SCOTLAND: folklore 8-9
SCOTT, ESTHER HAYS: first wife of Richard Powell 79
SEALS, ROBERT M. (journalist): 94-95
SEELEY, KENNETH: establishes Bell Witch Opry 86
SEELEY, NINA: establishes Bell Witch Opry 86; 114
SETTLEMENT: whites defy law 4
SEVIER, JOHN: dislike for Andrew Jackson 46
SICKNESS: on frontier 39-40
SLAVES: on Bell farm 13; witch's opinion of 59, 60; South's attitude toward 60
SMALLPOX: Andrew Jackson contracts 44
SMITHLAND (Ky.): 12
SPIDER, brown recluse: in Bell Witch Cave 100
SPRINGFIELD (Tenn.): 50
SPROUSE, MARY RICHARDS: xiv
ST. HELENA ISLAND: 68
STATE CAPITOL (Nashville): built on Indian mound 3
STORYTELLING: 8
STRAUB, PETER (author): 95

T
TALLAPOOSA RIVER (Ga.): 47
TARBORO (N. C.): 9
TAYLOR, TRAILL (president of Royal Photographic Society of England): researches spirit photos xi-xiii
TENNESSEAN, THE: 100